LONDON PRIDE

LONDON PRIDE

Etchings by Nance Lui Fyson

Text by Aubrey Noakes

JUPITER : LONDON

First published in 1978 by
JUPITER BOOKS (LONDON) LIMITED
167 Hermitage Road, London N4.

Etchings © Nance Lui Fyson 1978.
Text © Jupiter Books (London) Limited 1978.

ISBN O 904041 79 4 CASED
ISBN O 904041 94 8 LIMP

Composed in 10-point Monotype Bembo, Series 270,
by Ronset Limited, Darwen, Lancashire.
Printed and bound in Great Britain.
By Penshurst Press Limited.

PREFACE BY NANCE LUI FYSON

London, an ugly place indeed! We soon discovered that it abounded in delightful nooks and corners; in picturesque scenes and groups; in light and shade of the most attractive character. The work-a-day life of the metropolis, that to the careless or inartistic eye is hard, angular, and ugly in its exterior aspects, offered us pictures at every street corner . . .

GUSTAVE DORE AND BLANCHARD JERROLD, *London, A Pilgrimage* (1872).

EARLY NINETEENTH-CENTURY LONDON is well recorded in attractive prints and pictures. But by the 1860s it was regarded as an ugly, smoke-laden place. Novels, social studies, and sketches of the period portrayed the seamy side of life in the big city, especially that of the poor. The quotation above from the 1870s is somehow strikingly apt today. There is again that feeling that London is becoming an ugly place.

Many books published in the 1970s, with titles like *Goodbye London*, have bemoaned the changing face of the city. Redevelopment has often meant bland glass and concrete replacing a finely textured scene. The muddle of the streets, with juxtapositions of detailed and varied buildings, old street fixtures and signs, is being tidied-up in many places. The resulting efficiency and smoothness is at the expense of that hard-to-define but cherished aspect of the urban environment – *character*.

What follows are reproduced etchings that were based on drawings made in the streets, markets, and parks of London in the mid-1970s. There is no attempt to show the twentieth century equivalent of the exercise yard at Newgate Prison, the wretched homeless children and other scenes of squalor and depression so vividly shown in the engravings of Doré.

Here is simply an affectionate view of the picturesque – some of the delightful muddle of people and places that gives London its character. When drawn, The Delightful Muddle antique shop (see frontispiece) in Pimlico was scheduled for demolition. The delightful muddle of London is well worth trying to keep.

CONTENTS

INTRODUCTION BY AUBREY NOAKES

MANY AUTHORS SAY they never read reviews of their books, I always do. One can learn something, even if it is only that the reviewers have read the blurb (which one may have written or prepared one-self) and not the book! But, seriously, writing is such a *solitary* business no author can know if he has succeeded until he gets a few reactions from somewhere or somebody about his work. As a confessed reader of my own reviewers I cherish one gem from Henry Williamson: 'Mr. Noakes is a good friend to artists.' He was reviewing an early work of mine, *The World of Henry Alken* (1952).

But just as the morning and evening newspapers could inspire Offenbach, and Teutonic legend could impel Wagner to deafen us all with the mesmeric force of his genius, so paintings and drawings get me going as a writer, and, as I remarked in the Henry Alken book, quoting Hazlitt, the great advantage the artist has over the writer is that he, or in this case, she, Nance Lui Fyson, can make her point *instantaneously* – there 'tis! You can take in her message in one gulp, whereas the writer has to bumble on, relying for his effect upon a series of cumulative strokes, a piling of word upon word, creating a succession of verbal images, searching frantically for the right word, wrestling with problems of syntax and heaven knows what else, to achieve a like result, *communicate* an idea or information.

Moreover, I could not agree more with Alice: 'What use is a book without pictures!' I have loved the illustrated book since I was a child. Not only am I lost in admiration at the artist's work, but a shade envious, too, and never more so than when confronted with that of one who can both write *and* draw. I was brought up on Charles G. Harper's *Road* books and loved the drawings with which he casually peppers and salts his text. One of my favourite books by him is *Cycle Rides Round London* (1902), which inspired him (legitimately) to even get a little boastful. He describes it on the title-page as 'Ridden, Written and Illustrated' by Charles G. Harper. Follow *that*, as they say!

However, all that is by way of prolegomena to my Introduction. We know people, and may be guilty ourselves, banging on about modern architecture, about packing people into high-rise, box-styled blocks of flats or towering office-blocks, and about conveyor-belt driving on the motor-ways which streamline traffic but violate the landscape. And at the rate we are progressing, one major city will soon look much like another. So runs the argument, as summarised in the globe-trotter's question and answer routine: Startled Airways Passenger, on waking: 'Where are we, miss?' Bored Air-Hostess, answering the same tom-fool question for the umpteenth time: 'It's Wednesday, must be Copenhagen.'

Well, what Nance Lui Fyson does in her engaging, unpretentious way is to prove that no one could mistake London, England, for anywhere else. It still has bags of character and endless surprises in store for anyone who cares to move around a bit and use their eyes. She has not set out to make an exhaustive, systematic survey of London, but simply loitered here and there on her sketching forays to capture for our delight some aspect of the London scene that has caught her fancy.

My delight is to introduce Nance Lui Fyson's London, but her drawings do that for themselves; so my task fines itself down to introducing London. In doing so I cannot do better than reiterate the message of the drawings themselves, namely that London is endlessly fascinating, it has something new to say about her dear self every day to those with alert, wondering minds and a determination never to be bored.

As Dr Johnson said, and he said so many wise and true things: 'A man who is tired of London is tired of life.' Heard *that* before? All right, but few seem to recall his follow-up: 'Sir, if you wish to have a just notion of the magnitude of this City, you must not be satisfied with seeing its great streets and squares, but must survey the innumerable little lanes and courts. It is not in the showy evolutions of her buildings, but in the multiplicity of human habitations, which are crowded together that the wonderful immensity of London consists.'

Nance Fyson has clearly read the doctor's prescription since it will be noted how London personalities, like Mr Hart in Leather Lane, the solo musician in Cecil Court, the group around Tubby Isaacs' stall, and the pavement artist at Hyde Park all figure as much as the buildings and streets in her drawings. As she sees it, they are as much an integral part of the 'London mix' as any of its grand buildings.

Again, as Dr Johnson said to Boswell at dinner in The Mitre in Fleet Street (now, alas! marked only by one of those familiar blue plaques) on the evening of 30 September 1769: 'I will venture to say, there is more learning and science within the circumference of ten miles from where we now sit, than in all the rest of the kingdom.' So, unless you *are* tired of life, and wish to vegetate, why leave London? Friends think me a trifle eccentric when I say London is a place to retire *to*, not get out of. Let me explain, and I can best do so in personal terms.

As a writer I have had the pleasure of haunting art galleries and museums for over forty years, usually for the press or private view of a forthcoming exhibition, about which I have had to write something for a magazine or newspaper. Few have the time in a workaday life to do much of that – but, when they retire? They have *all the time in the world*! They will be surprised to find what is on offer in London's museums and galleries: special lectures and film shows, and all free. There are societies and clubs scattered about London, too, which cover most interests, *and* your special ones, more likely than not. The desire to get out of town for a holiday or a week-end break makes sense when one leads a busy, workaday life, but I wonder sometimes if it is all that wise to cut oneself off from one's working past in the evening of life and often to places where one hardly knows anybody.

The rage of the elderly to do so and crowd the coastal resorts of Devon and Cornwall, for example, puts such a strain on the local medical service that doctors now designate such areas in their dog-Latin as the *costa geriatica*. Mind you, there are times when people have things to do which may, with justice, be thought preferable to rambling about London. Boswell visited Johnson towards the close of the doctor's life (Saturday, 12 April 1783) in company with William Windham M.P., and Johnson talked a great deal on that favourite topic of his, the wonderful extent and variety of London. He observed that 'men of curious enquiry might see in it such modes of life as very few could even imagine. He in particular recommended to us to *explore Wapping*, which we resolved to do.'

That was all very fine, but Windham, who was an ardent fight-fan and devotee of all traditional English sports, was less than charmed about this Wapping expedition. In his *Diary* he wrote: 'I let myself foolishly be drawn by Boswell to explore, as he called it, Wapping, instead of going when everything was prepared, to see the battle between Ward and Stanyard, which turned out a very good one and which would have served as a very good introduction to Boswell.'

Glancing over the last paragraph or so, we agree, there has been an awful lot about Johnson. This has been quite deliberate. The subject of London is so vast, and since one must start somewhere, why not *personalise* your studies? If Boswell's biography of his friend happens to be a favourite book of yours, why not then, start there: follow up the London references in the *Life*. Then there is Boswell's own *London Journal 1762–63*, not to mention all the subsequent volumes of his journals that keep coming out, and in which he explores not only Wapping but every fleeting thought that passes through his mind and chronicles his exploits, too, in Proustian detail. This should supply you with a very solid base upon which to build your future London studies.

From that point you can move forward or backwards. Please yourself, it is *your* show. Forward to an exploration of the London of Dickens and the other great Victorian novelists, or, back to seventeenth century London, to the London of Pepys and Evelyn, of London before the Great Fire (1666) and afterwards, when Wren rebuilt St Paul's and so many more City churches. Discover too, how importantly the City loomed during the Civil War.

Fond of the theatre? Well, get lost in Southwark, the Southwark Shakespeare knew, and of the Globe Theatre. Find out what sort of lives the Elizabethan actors led. One of them, Edward Allelyn, founded Dulwich College and some of his companions must have liked that part of the world too, since that delectable south London suburb contains many streets named after players and colleagues of Shakespeare, there is *Henslowe* Road, *Burbage* Road, *Alleyn* Park. Your study of Shakespeare's Southwark will merge with your earlier Dickens studies: Dickens all over the place in Southwark, the George Inn, the 'Little Dorrit' church, Lant Street, the site of the old Marshalsea prison. Study the coaching inns of Southwark, as Mr Pickwick knew them, and where in the courtyard of one of them found Sam Weller; this will bring to your notice the Tabard Inn from whence Chaucer's pilgrims set out for Canterbury and the shrine of St Thomas Becket, another great citizen of medieval London, like Chaucer himself.

Interested? Read *Chaucer's London* (1968) by D. W. Robertson, a detailed account of all aspects of City life in the fourteenth century, complete with maps and illustrations. And, if you want to go further back and know something of the even earlier London that Thomas Becket knew, you are very much in luck, since William Fitzstephen, who was Becket's chaplain and a horrified witness of his martyrdom in Canterbury Cathedral, set to and wrote the biography of his master four years later, just after Thomas' speedy canonization. A Londoner himself, and clearly proud of it, Fitzstephen sets the scene for the agonising story he had to tell by describing vividly the London in which Becket was born and reared, and few London anthologies miss quoting from him.

Becket's martyrdom came after years of uneasy relations with his sovereign and erstwhile companion, Henry II, and perforce, this great Londoner spent many years in exile. French Railways put out a special brochure for English pilgrims to Becket's French homes and see. He was created in his time, not only Archbishop of Canterbury, but Bishop of Sens, too, and his mitre, as Bishop of Sens can be seen in a glass case in the Victoria and Albert Museum, there on permanent loan from the Cardinal Archbishop of Westminster. The first of these, Cardinal Wiseman, brought the mitre back to this country.

Consideration of the London of Becket and Chaucer leads us to a study of the religious life of what some writers have termed the Age of Faith, when London was rich in churches and religious foundations: the great hospital of St Bartholemew was founded by a courtier-turned-monk, Rahere, and the vast church of St Bartholemew was served by Augustinian canons. Fortunately, this was one of the churches Wren did not need to do much about. It escaped the Great Fire (1666), and as you loiter in its vast interior you can muse on the religious life of London when the realm was part of Christendom and its archbishops received the pallium as token of their communion with the see of St Peter in Rome. London place-names recall those times and the presence within it of the great religious orders: Blackfriars, Whitefriars, Carthusian Street, Carmelite Street, Paternoster Row, Ave Maria Lane.

Read Dom David Knowles' magisterial works on the religious orders and their houses in medieval England, and especially the one he did on the London Charterhouse in collaboration with Professor W. F. Grimes, in which is recorded the story of the exciting archaeological 'finds' on the site in post-War London.

And, of course, if you have been thrilled by the news of these finds, the Temple of Mithras and the rest, you can study the foundation of the City – LONDINIUM – and discover how our forbears became part of the far-flung Roman Empire.

If your interests are more contemporary get hold of Ian Nairn's *Modern Buildings in London* (a London Transport publication) next time you buy a red or green Rover ticket. 'Without any doubt, London is one of the best cities in the world for modern architecture,' writes Ian Nairn. 'But it is also one of the biggest cities in the world, and it does not make a display of its best things. A visitor looking for new buildings in the City and the West End might well be justified in turning away with a shudder. Yet delightful things may be waiting for him in Lewisham or St. Albans.' His book will help you to find them and he describes in some detail 250 of them. An architectural correspondent of *The Observer* he has also produced an offbeat guide to London generally, *Nairn's London*. Get it, and keep it alongside your Ward Lock or Blue Guide, and the invaluable *A–Z Street Guide*.

And, although we have listed and briefly described some of the many, many volumes that have been written and produced about London in the select list at the end of the book, remember, that much of the best writing on London is to be found buried away in autobiographies where the famous describe their early days. Thus, Harold Macmillan, sometime Prime Minister and for many years an active member of his family's publishing firm, has a wonderful passage in the first volume of his memoirs in which he describes his London childhood. In the nursery of a house off Sloane Street he used to gaze out of the window into a mews where a fire blazed permanently, there was a blacksmith's workshop serving the late Victorian London of horse-drawn traffic he so vividly recalls, when straw was laid out before a house where a duchess lay ill to deaden the noise of traffic. Thomas Burke, of *Limehouse Nights* fame, whom I had the pleasure of knowing, maintained that London was a much noiser place then than it is in the age of the motor-car.

Talk to some of the old folk you will meet in those London taverns, which Nance Lui Fyson has drawn with such skill and taste, and get them to tell you about the London they knew when they began work, or what school was like in their childhood.

A proper cockney, William Hogarth, very much a self-made man and proud of it, grew up in an atmosphere of trade in the heart of the City and began his artistic career as a designer and engraver of shop-cards. When he was portrayed in a crowd before the Guildhall in an engraving entitled *A Stir in the City* (1754) everyone recognised the stumpy, independent little fellow. Many London sites figure as topographical backgrounds in Hogarth's engravings. But although Hogarth's upbringing was far from modish and elegant it would be quite misleading to regard him as an untutored genius. He rather overdid the 'boiled beef and carrots, and no nonsense' plain-man's stuff, and as much of his work in the Tate Gallery shows, he could essay the grand manner with the best of his contemporaries. He revelled in controversy, rather like Munnings in our own time, but, as he once playfully confided to Mrs Piozzi: 'The Connoisseurs and I are at war, you know; and because I hate them, they think I hate Titian, and let 'em!'

Study Hogarth, Samuel Scott and Canaletto's Thames-side scenes, Whistler's nocturnes, and, indeed, the London scenes of all the great artists; the books on London's theatres, past and present, by those indefatigable researchers, Mander and Mitchenson, and the histories of individual theatres by the late W. MacQueen Pope. There is no end to the angles from which you can approach your London studies. Surprisingly enough, to some people, it is a great place for naturalists, with its wide, open spaces, its former royal parks, and one of my own favourite books is *Richard Jeffries London* (nicely illustrated with drawings), edited by S. J. Looker, in which is gathered together much of Jeffries' London writings.

As a schoolboy I used to hear lectures about London at the Horniman Museum, Forest Hill, SE23, given by a Mr Roberts. These were accompanied with a wealth of slides, many of them from photographs he took himself, and he rattled on, full of enthusiasm and non-stop for about 70 minutes flat . . . and then, he would wind up, invariably thus; '. . . but nowhere can the spirit of London at any period of its history be more authentically recaptured than in song.' And, before anyone could catch their breath, he was off, with a rich concert-party baritone voice. If he had been telling us about Shakespeare's London it would be a madrigal or some enchanting setting to a song from *Twelfth Night*; the eighteenth century would elicit from him a melody from Thomas Tickell's repertoire, or maybe Tony Lumpkin's song. A stunned, but delighted audience staggered out into the street, lost in admiration for a man who could suddenly burst into song after talking non-stop for well over an hour.

Well, *you* have Nance Lui Fyson's etchings, but the publishers simply will not stand for me throwing in a give-away record album, and, quite frankly, it would be redundant anyway. Linger with Nance's subtle and masterly etchings and you will see why.

LONDON PRIDE

I. SHEPHERDS MARKET, WI.

Here we are in the heart of Mayfair. In 1735 Edward Shepherd founded the market 'for the buying and selling of flesh, fish, fowl, roots, herbs, and other provisions for human food,' on the plot of ground where an annual May Fair was once held. The fair consisted originally of a goods and cattle market and was first held in 1688, but became so rowdy and notorious that it was formally banned in 1708 although it appears to have kept going in an undercover, surreptitious kind of way for some years after this.

Curio shops mingle with cafes and pubs in a village atmosphere only a stone's-throw away from the prestigious thoroughfares of Piccadilly, Curzon Street, and Park Lane.

2. CECIL COURT, WC2.

If you have walked the boots off yourself in search of that out-of-print book you want in Charing Cross
Road, and had no luck, not to worry, try Cecil Court. During the 1930s twenty-two bookshops lined
this court which lies between St Martin's Lane and Charing Cross Road, and there was some talk of
having it renamed, American-fashion, Booksellers' Row, but nothing came of it, which may be as well
since there are fewer bookshops there these days. However, those which are there are always worth a
visit. The court takes it name from Sir Robert Cecil (later created the Earl of Salisbury), Lord High
Treasurer under James I. The busker with the recorder shown in the drawing plays a fine selection of
Bach and old folk tunes, and is as much part of the 'scene' as the shops themselves.

3. FLASK WALK, HAMPSTEAD, NW3.

The Flask Tavern, from which the Walk takes its name, was built in 1767. Health-giving waters, taken from a well in Well Walk, were prepared and distributed from Flask Walk all over London. Messengers were required to return their empty flasks daily.

4. BREWERS LANE, RICHMOND, SURREY.

The lane appears in the Court Rolls in 1608, and is one of Richmond's oldest thoroughfares. Earlier records show that it was called Magpye Lane, after the name of a tavern which was there in the seventeenth century; but as there were several other taverns in the lane, too, but long since vanished, it became known later as Brewers Lane and the name has stuck.

5. MIDDLESEX STREET, EI — PETTICOAT LANE.

This has been London's best-known Sunday market for a century now. 'Going dahn the Lane', is a parting phrase heard by many a Mum as she potters around clearing the breakfast table for male members of her family. Naturally, they will expect her to have lunch ready when they get back!

Difficult to believe it when one looks at 'the Lane' today but back in the fourteenth century it was a straggling country lane known as Berwardes Lane, after a local landowner. In the sixteenth century it changed to Hog Lane, because of the surrounding pig farms; and again, in the seventeenth century, to Petticoat Lane, on account of the old-clothes dealers who began to congregate there. The present somewhat misleading name for visitors, who seek in vain in their street guides for 'Petticoat Lane', comes from the county. Most of London north of the Thames was in Middlesex before the formation of the County of London.

It is a lively colourful scene and it is well worth waiting for a nice spring or summer morning for your excursion 'dahn the Lane.' Since the top end of Middlesex Street comes out near 'Dirty Dick's,' if you are unfamiliar with the East End, simply make for Liverpool Street Station or Bishopsgate. There will be crowds about and anyone will tell you where the 'Lane is.

21

6. LEATHER LANE, EC1.

A curious thoroughfare, this, which figures in John Stow's *Survey* (1603) as 'Lither Lane'. Place-name enthusiasts can have a lot of fun – and they have! – in arguing over its original name and meaning. Most agree, though, that the present form is corrupt. 'Louerone Lane' is the earliest recorded form, we believe, and this appears in the Calendar of Wills in the Court of Hustings in 1306. The old French *leveroun*, a greyhound, figures in the endless discussions, with its 'gay dog' associations (cf. 'levron': a pleasure-seeking young man).

However we doubt if these philological niceties much worry lunch-hour shoppers as they bustle about looking for bargains, listening to the stall-holders' patter, and between whiles keeping a sharp eye on their watches to ensure they get back to their offices punctually after their welcome break.

Maybe, modern super-markets *are* much more efficient, but they lack the colour of the street-markets and their rich crop of personalities, such as E. Hart (born 1898) shown here in his dark anorak at his stall in 'the Lane'. He has been bringing cardboard boxes full of men's clothes to his stall here since 1929. After the first World War his mother took him to a phrenologist who suggested that there was a great future for the lad in the colonies. So, off he went to Canada, where, amongst other things, he swept floors in Winnipeg, and performed as a diver in a circus.

7. CRAVEN STREET, STRAND, WC2.

Like so many street names this one, too, is a reminder of past days; of the time when the wealthy Craven family owned much of the land thereabouts and its members included Sir William Craven, the merchant tailor who rose to become Lord Mayor of London. There are many old houses in the street, including one, marked by a plaque, where Benjamin Franklin once lived. Dickens enthusiasts will recall that it was in his lodgings in this street that Mr Brownlow had the interview with Rose Maylie that resulted in the recovery of Oliver Twist; and, at the bottom, on the site now covered by the railway station, stood old Hungerford Market, and the blacking-warehouse where Dickens worked for a short time as a boy.

The flower seller depicted here outside Charing Cross Station has been part of the local 'scenery' for as many years as we can recall.

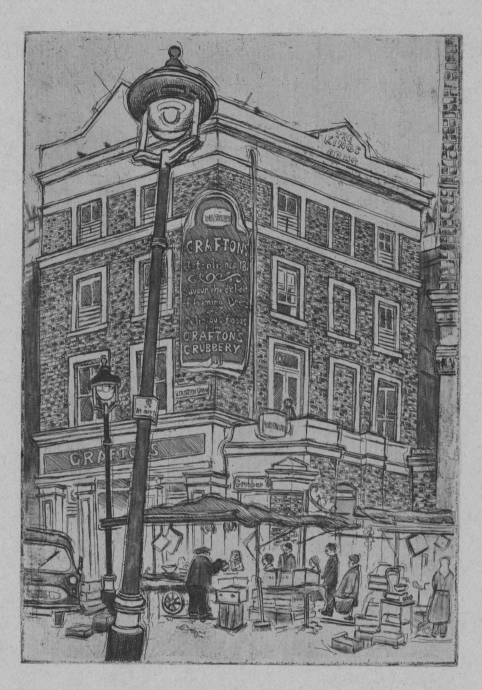

8. STRUTTON GROUND, SWI.

'Stourton Ground' was once the ground or meadow which lay behind Stourton House, the town residence of Lord Stourton. The name came to be given to the path beside the meadow, and got changed by the vagaries of pronunciation over the years to 'Strutton Ground'. Traders claim that it is the oldest street market in the country, with daily stalls doing a brisk trade in fruit, vegetables, and flowers both with residents of the huge blocks of flats in the area and with office-workers from Victoria Street, and from whom most traders will accept luncheon-vouchers as readily as money. The foundations and identifiable portions of a number of buildings and houses in Strutton Ground can be traced back to Tudor or Stuart days; and, what naturally attracts the attention of the artist is that this (village-type) market is to be found scarcely a stone's-throw away from the Army and Navy Stores in Victoria Street. Indeed, you walk out of Victoria Street right into Strutton Ground at the top end.

9. MOOR STREET, SOHO, WI.

Difficult to believe that the name Soho derived from a hunting call once heard in the open fields thereabouts, but that was before Red's time. 'Red', the ginger-haired soft-spoken Irish seller of soft drinks
and snacks has worked in Soho streets for over twenty years. It is a curious, faintly sinister area, but the
only one in which certain types of food and delicacies can be obtained in London, and many of the
traders there have been resident for three or four generations in the area.

25

10. LONDON'S OLDEST PAVEMENT ARTIST.

II. TUBBY ISAACS', GOULSTON STREET, EI.

'We Lead, Others Follows.' Thus spake Tubby, 'Famous for Jellied Eeels.' The Tubby Isaacs stall has become a built-in feature in the East End since 1928. East End boys who have made it to the top – dance-band leaders at the ritziest hotels in the West End – have been known to drive in style in limousines down to Tubby's to relive the youthful thrill of a bowl or plateful of Tubby's 'speciality of the day.' The present owner is the brother-in-law of the original Tubby.

12. BAYSWATER ROAD, W2.

This thoroughfare runs from Marble Arch to Notting Hill Gate on the north side of Hyde Park and Kensington Gardens. Situated on land which once belonged to Bairnardus of Normandy and fed by a water supply called Bairnardus' or Baynard's Watering, the area has since become known as Bayswater. One great feature of this stretch of road in recent years has been the development of a Sunday open-air art market in which we find on display, leather goods, painting, pottery, old prints tastefully framed, jewellery, pottery and other kinds of *obiet d'art*. Rentals for these 'show cases' need to be obtained from the Westminster City Council by would-be vendors, who, in many cases are the artists or craftsmen themselves, and who find this a convenient and relatively inexpensive way to bring their work to the notice of the public.

13. OLD CASTLE STREET, E1.

Children determined to 'educate their masters' will *arrange matters* next time they go 'dahn the Lane' so that Dad's footsteps can be guided a street or so further on towards the roasted peanuts stand in Old Castle Street, by Aldgate East Tube Station. Recommend the nuts and ice cold drinks with an air of authority, as though you were doing Dad a favour in letting him in on a great secret. He should feel privileged to pay! If Dad is not around, try it out on Mum. Tougher work, that, but it has been known to succeed. For evidence of this, see the drawing accompanying. 'Childish Guile Rewarded.' How's that for a caption?

14. VICTORIA, SW1.

With the sensational news-making headlines the other day about an American bid to buy Victoria Station our caption is ready-made here, surely? 'Wanna buy a paper or the station, son?'

15. SOUTHAMPTON ROW, WC1.

This thoroughfare leading from Russell Square to Kingsway forms one of the most important arteries between North and South London and is named after Thomas Wriothesley, fourth Earl of Southampton, whose father had been Shakespeare's patron. His estate was divided by lot and his daughter, Rachel (1636–1723), whose husband, William Lord Russell was involved in the Rye House Plot, got part of the manor of Bloomsbury and St Giles, with Southampton House and an estate in Hampshire. John, 13th and present Duke of Bedford, in his none too reverent contribution to family history, *A Silver-Plated Spoon* (1959) comments: 'It was considered at the time that she had got the worst of the bargain, but as we are still living precariously off the proceeds of the Bloomsbury estate today, I have no cause for complaint.' Let's leave it there.

The large watch displayed in the drawing opposite has been on show in the Row since World War I and hung outside the Waltham Watch Factory in High Holborn before that: a welcome survival, this, of the old custom of exhibiting trade signs to let people know what you are all about.

31

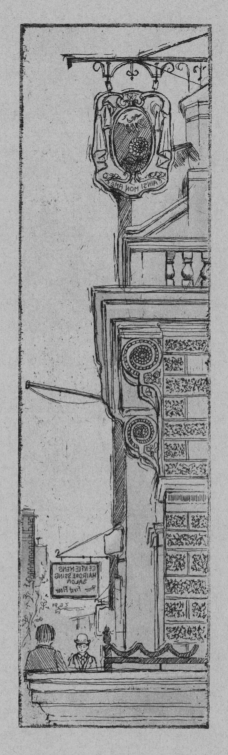

16. CHILD'S BANK, FLEET STREET, EC4.

The Bank's origins can be traced back to William Wheeler, who set up as a goldsmith in the 'Chepe' (later Cheapside) in 1559. His descendants moved to No. 1 Fleet Street to carry on their business there as goldsmiths and bankers 'at the Sign of the Marigold.' There had been a tavern of that name there and the Wheelers and the Childs shrewdly adopted the old sign as their own; the bank's cheques became famous for their own marigold watermark.

17. MARBLE ARCH, W1.

Designed by John Nash, the favourite architect of George IV, and inspired by the Arch of Constantine in Rome, it is made from Carrara marble and once formed the entrance to Buckingham Palace, but it was moved in 1851 since it was found that state carriages could not easily negotiate the centre arch. Believe it or not, that statue of George IV by Chantrey which you see in Trafalgar Square today, was suggested as a further 'something has been added' adornment to the arch in its Buckingham Palace days!

Nearby is the famous (or infamous?) site of Tyburn Tree (last used in 1783) where martyrs, highwaymen and murderers alike met their savage and barbarous ends by hanging.

18. LONDON'S LAST TOLL GATE, DULWICH VILLAGE, SE21.

It is, as they say, strange but true that the last existing toll-gate in London is to be found in Dulwich Village, scarcely five miles from the centre of town. The road in which it stands is known now as College Road although when the road was first formed in 1804 it was known as Morgan's Road, then it became Penge Road, before College Road was finally settled upon. The Table of Tolls is amusing to read these days. As a concession to twentieth century *innovations* they *do* include motor vehicles in the list, but keep in the list charges for 'every horse, mule or donkey drawing any vehicle', 'beasts per score', 'lambs, sheep or hogs, per score.'

If you are intrigued by the manner in which the Estates Governors of 'Alleyn's College of God's Gift' (Dulwich College) resisted pressure from nineteenth century property developers and so helped preserve Dulwich from the urban sprawl which settled like a blight elsewhere, read all about it in *Victorian Suburb*, by H. J. Dyos (1961).

19. CARTING LANE, WC2.

The drawing shows the famous gas lamp in Carting Lane which is always alight. The lamp is lit from gases in the sewers beneath the streets. For centuries this thoroughfare was known as Dirty Lane, up to about 1830, that is. It was probably the route for carts bringing goods from the wharfs at the bottom of the lane.

Note the side-entrance at the foot of the stairs to the Coal Hole tavern in the Strand, and the sign above the stairs directing people to the Savoy Theatre, the entrance to which is in the forecourt of the Savoy Hotel. The theatre was built and opened by D'Oyly Carte in October 1881 as a home for the Gilbert and Sullivan operas, which were produced there continuously from 1881 to 1889. *Journey's End* was first produced there on 21 January 1929, and Sheridan Morley owes his name to the fact that his distinguished father, Robert Morley, was playing the part there of the insufferable Sheridan Whiteside in *The Man Who Came to Dinner* when he was born.

20. THE FULHAM POTTERY, SW6.

Founded 1672, the pottery was set up by a certain John Dwight, who patented his experiments with clay. The 300-years-old bottle kiln in the courtyard is what remains from the original pottery established there, and it never fails to catch the eyes of passers-by.

21. THE MONUMENT, EC3.

Sir Christopher Wren (1632–1723) was so modest he did his boasting in Latin! His self-supplied epitaph in St Paul's, *Lector, si monumentum reqiris, circumspice* may be freely translated thus: 'Reader, I don't want to talk about myself, but this is *it*! All my own work! Look around!' Quite so! But Wren did have a hand in rebuilding a few other City churches too, and there is no better place to get a bird's-eye view of them all than from the top of the Monument. Wren designed this also, although its detailed execution was left to Robert Hooke, the City architect.

Built of Portland stone 'The Monument' is a fluted Doric column, 15 ft. diameter and 202 ft. high. It stands in a small open square known as Monument yard on the east side of Fish Street Hill. There are stacks of monuments all over London, of course, but this is invariably referred to as 'The Monument'. It was built to mark the spot nearby – a baker's shop in Pudding Lane – where the Great Fire (1666) broke out. Do not miss the brave, baroque splendour of the sculptured panel on the west side of the monument, which is the work of Caius Gabriel Cibber. In view of present land values in the City it is amusing to learn that in 1673 payment of five guineas for tithe was made to the Rector of St Margaret's, Fish Street Hill, in respect of the ground whereon The Monument stands.

22. THE OLD ROMAN WALL AT THE BARBICAN, EC3.

Never mind that stuff about London being built by a Trojan refugee named Brutus and designated 'New Troy', and then later getting itself rechristened London after an equally legendary character, King Lud. These tales derive from medieval chroniclers like Geoffrey of Monmouth and do not stand up to hard scrutiny. In the Royal Commission Report of 1928 the late Sir Mortimer Wheeler declared 'there is no valid reason for supposing that London existed prior to A.D.43.'

In spite of the great strides made since then in archaeological studies this statement remains unchallenged. Thus you cannot begin your London studies at a better place than with Roman London, and with rambles round the City where parts of the Roman wall can be found. Follow up with visits to the appropriate galleries in the Museum of London close by, and supplement these with visits to the superb collection of Roman antiquities in the British Museum. The excellent official publications in both places, specially written by scholars for the general public, constitute the best moneysworth still in this field. Their bibliographies should help as a guide to further study.

The Wall was about 3 and 1/8th miles in circuit and enclosed an irregular oblong of 330 acres. It survived well after its military purpose had become an irrelevance. In the late eighteenth century it was razed because it hampered building development and traffic. Fragments seen above ground are medieval renewals and heightenings of the Roman wall; the Roman work is fifteen feet or so below the surface. One of the ironies of World War II bombing is, that whilst it caused loss of life and property in the City, it also, unwittingly, helped solve many problems which had puzzled archaeologists and historians for centuries.

23. LINCOLN'S INN GATEWAY, CHANCERY LANE, WC2.

Lincoln's Inn is one of the four great Inns of Court. The others are Gray's Inn, Holborn; and the Inner and Middle Temple. These four 'Societies' are governed by Benchers, who alone have the authority to call students 'to the bar', i.e. to formally pronounce them to be 'Barristers of this Inn.' We have stressed the 'nooks and corners' aspect of London in this book, naturally, since that is what many of the drawings are about, but the four Inns do help illustrate this aspect of London life in a quite telling way. Many visitors being shown over them for the first time remark how reminiscent they are of the quadrangles and squares of Oxford and Cambridge colleges, and so they are, since in themselves they constitute London's own and ancient University of Law, with elaborate rules and traditions of their own. The literature on them all is quite vast and forms a rewarding area of study in itself.

24. BERKELEY SQUARE, WI.

This is the square where the nightingale allegedly sang and the setting of one of our favourite plays, *Berkeley Square*, by John L. Balderston, suggested by Henry James's 'The Sense of Time.' Landsdowne House has disappeared, of course, but there are blue plaques all over the place to remind us of who lived where and when in its prestigious past. Several original Georgian mansions survive on the west side of the square, including No. 45, once the home of Lord Clive of Plassey. Our illustration shows one of the surviving features of such mansions: the trumpet-shaped link extinguishers which were used for snuffing out burning tapers carried by servants to light their master on his way, and very necessary before the introduction of street lighting. Link boys scurried about for custom outside theatres or any great house where a great ball, rout, or 'assembly' was going forward. Note the fine craftsmanship which distinguishes much of the ironwork and look out for further examples as you move around London, and, indeed, the country.

25. PIERREPONT ARCADE, N1.

A lightning glimpse here of the arcade which forms part of the Camden Passage Antique Market which has developed on a severely bombed-out site since the end of the Second World War. Concrete and awnings for Pierrepont and Charlton Markets were laid in 1960 by John Friend and Associates. The market has also attracted a number of dealers to settle in the area.

26. PORTOBELLO ROAD, WII.

Originally a pleasant country lane leading to Portobello Farm. The road's curious name, incidentally, celebrates Admiral Vernon's victory at Puerto Bello in the Gulf of Mexico against the Spanish in 1739. Vernon was less successful later in his expedition against Cartagena (1741) in which Tobias Smollett served as a surgeon's-mate. The shocking conditions in the British Navy then are described in his novel, *Roderick Random*. But enough of that.

To judge from old newspaper files the late Victorian market in Portobello Road was quite something: an untidy mix-up of costermongers, stall-holders, itinerant entertainers, conjurors, flame-eaters, and 'London characters' straight out of Mayhew. The antique set-up we find there today only seems to have got off the ground in the 1950s although Dan (seen in the drawing here) claims that he has been around since 1949! His great speciality is those status symbols so beloved by the Mr Pooters of yesteryear: the gold watch-chains jauntily referred to as 'Alberts', and he deals more with other traders in the market, really, than the public, like so many dealers we find. Further north in the market there is a medley of furniture dealers, fruit sellers, old clothes dealers, and bric-a-brac specialists.

27. BILLINGSGATE MARKET, EC3.

Billingsgate, the City of London's fish market, is of ancient origin, and one suspects was so, long before the earliest known medieval Charters and Acts of Parliament were drawn up authorising the Corporation to conduct a free and open market for the sale of fish. A recent check shows that about 110 firms operate in the market and employ about 2,500 people. But, one needs to get up early in the morning to see the market in action. This goes on for a pretty lively three to four hours, after which the market is thoroughly cleansed and washed down daily. A curious peace descends on the area then, in quite marked contrast to the early morning bustle.

The first Royal Charter referring to the market was issued by Edward I in 1297, but the present fish-market you see (like Smithfield and Leadenhall markets) was designed by Sir Horace Jones, the City architect, in 1876, to replace the old sheds and stalls and bring it up-to-date. On normal trading days about 250 tons of fish are handled. The market-porters in their traditional flat-top leather hats and white smocks enliven the scene greatly . . . and, to put it discreetly, they are not a mealy-mouthed lot! To 'talk Billingsgate' may be best interpreted as indulging in *colourful* talk. Let's leave it at that!

43

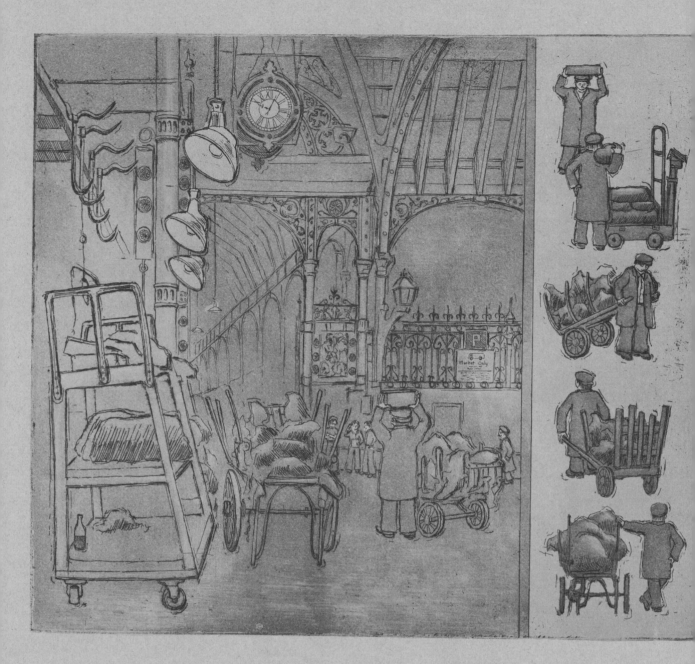

28. SMITHFIELD MARKET, EC1.

Smithfield Market, or to describe it formally, the Central Markets Committee of the Corporation of London, covers nearly ten acres around the 'smooth field' area medieval Londoners knew as a jousting-ground, just beyond the City's walls. The largest dead meat, poultry and provision market in the world today, it handles, according to the latest available figures, 350 million tons of produce annually.

Nevertheless, one of the most striking impressions visitors get as they stroll through the market after business hours is one of extreme cleanliness. It is hard to believe that, only a few hours before, the whole area was choked with lorries, with meat-porters (bummarees) weaving their way skilfully through the market, with great sides of beef draped carelessly over their shoulders, or manoevring their heavily-loaded barrows towards waiting lorries.

29. HENRIETTA STREET, COVENT GARDEN, WC2.

All right, we know what time of day it is, too! Covent Garden market moved to the Nine Elms in 1974? Right? But, before memory fades here is an impression of the old market just before it closed down. It is believed that the custom of selling fruit there can be traced back to medieval times when gardeners from the old Abbey at Westminster sold surplus produce in their own 'Convent Garden.' From such origins the market developed to become the key fruit, vegetable, and flower market in the United Kingdom, and one of the largest in the world.

Whilst the Nine Elms site has many advantages, no doubt, the four thousand porters, traders, and office staff employed at Covent Garden have felt a human and understandable tug at their heartstrings at the thought of leaving their old home. As one Covent Garden porter put it simply: 'It's very sad. It's a part of history going, isn't it? It'll be a different kind of life. . . .'

30. SPITALFIELDS MARKET, E1.

Strictly speaking, the Corporation of London's fruit and vegetable market and the adjoining flower market and fruit exchange at Spitalfields lie just outside the City's boundaries and in the London Borough of Tower Hamlets. However, they come under the control of the Spitalfields Market Committee of the Corporation with a Clerk and Superintendant responsible for day-to-day management.

The main market frontage stretches over 1½ miles and its stands are occupied by 150 wholesalers whilst two thousand people work in the market. There were thirty-six stands in the flower market at the last count.

In the twelfth century a hospital occupied the site, and from it's name, St Mary Spital, the name Spitalfields has evolved.

The term 'Spitalsfield silk' reminds us that some of the French Huguenots who came to this country after the Revocation of the Edict of Nantes settled in this part of London and brought their skills with them; and, much about the same time Spitalsfield developed as an early eighteenth-century New Town just beyond the City, and the irony of it is that although one can discover some isolated gems of eighteenth-century architecture and craftsmanship here and there in the area, no one seems much interested in rehabilitation and it looks as if the whole district, apart from the market, is doomed.

31. LEADENHALL MARKET, EC3.

Roofed with glass and lined with the premises of poultry and fish wholesalers this gas-lit, covered market is one of the most delightful curiosities and survivals of late Victorian London. Like Billingsgate and Smithfield Markets, this one, too, was designed by Sir Horace Jones, the City architect. Opened in 1881, it stands on the site of the Roman forum in the ancient city of Londinium. Getting a shade closer to our own day we find that the Corporation had an interest in the area in the fourteenth century when courts of justice were held occasionally at Leaden Hall.

Charles White states in the Corporation's own official guide that the inspiration for the market can be traced back to a black market in poultry in Edward III's time! He writes: 'In 1345 all strange folk bringing poultry into the City were ordered to take it to Leaden Hall for sale, and not to sell it in the lanes, the hostels, and elsewhere in secret at exorbitant prices.' City residents were advised to take their poultry to the stalls in West Cheap. In 1377 butter and cheese brought into the City had to be sold either at Leaden Hall or Newgate Market. Simon Eyre, the City's mayor in 1445–6, who built a granary at old Leaden Hall, as a kind of insurance against scarcity, figures in Thomas Dekker's play, *A Shoemaker's Holiday*.

Many a City worker, who, maybe, has to 'make do' with a cup of tea and a ham roll for his lunch on the day before pay day, can while away the time saved before he returns to his office by feasting his eyes wistfully upon rows of chickens and turkeys on hooks ascending dizzily roofwards, and a prodigious display of fish and fowl in this late Victorian paradise, Leadenhall Market. Hitler missed it, thank heaven! Let's hope no City bureaucrats ever plan it away!

47

32. WOOD STREET, CHEAPSIDE, EC2.

The Cheapside corner of Wood Street still has its plane tree and little shops beneath it. They mark the site of one of the churches which disappeared in the Great Fire (1666), St Peter's, West Cheap. This survival from late Victorian Cheapside, when many such business flourished thereabouts, is much appreciated since the area suffered very heavy damage in the Second World War. Indeed, from this end of Wood Street one could, just after the war, look straight down Wood Street, beyond the Gothic church-tower of St Alban's, 'spectral-white amid the havoc', and all that remained of it, over a ravaged site covering some 60-acres to the ruined church of St Giles', Cripplegate (since restored), where the poet, John Milton, lies buried.

Curiously enough, John Stow has little to say about St Alban's, although the medieval chronicler, Matthew Paris, tells us it was the chapel of King Offa in the eighth century. Thus a Christian foundation of some kind has occupied the site since early Saxon days. Inigo Jones restored or rebuilt it in 1633–4, and Wren, too, after the Great Fire, in 1682–7. It was so completely gutted in the last war, though, that it was decided to preserve only the Tower, which is certainly Wren's work, and the walls.

33. ST JAMES'S STREET, SWI.

A lovely bit of old London, this: Lock's, London's oldest hatters, founded in 1793, and to prove it they have an array of old hats in the window, including one older than the shop itself. An early patron was William Coke, who asked for a hat to be designed for him which we imagine was to be more of a crash helmet than an elegant piece of headwear. Dissatisfied with what the hatter came up with he threw it on the floor and jumped on it. The hat took on and became known as a 'billycock'; from this the City man and guards officers' off-duty bowler hat of today can trace descent.

34. NEW OXFORD STREET, WC1.

Note the display of the old trade sign outside the premises of James Smith & Sons, which was established in 1830 and is still owned by the family. The shop sells a bewildering variety of walking-sticks and umbrellas, including umbrellas with swords inside their handles. Irish blackthorns, malacca canes, man-about-town jobs for the white-tie-and-tail young men who have it in mind to step on stage and carry on from where Fred Astaire and Jack Buchanan left off, riding crops – you name it, they have it somewhere in their vast store. We have never passed this shop without noticing at least two or three people studying the contents of its window in a bemused, dazed fashion.

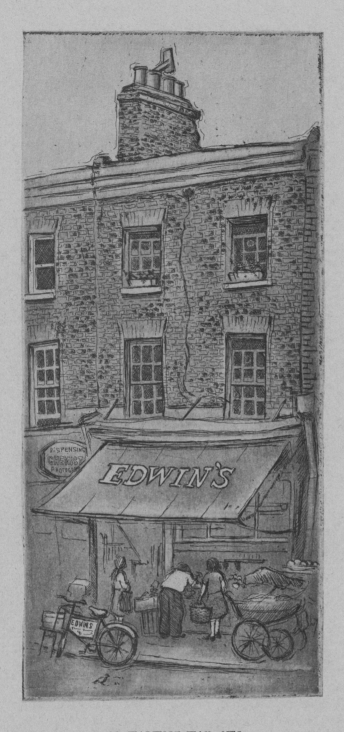

35. WARWICK WAY, SW1.

This was the earliest path across what was once the swampy wastes of Pimlico and it marked the track from Westminster Abbey to the Abbot's medieval country lodge. For centuries it was known as Willow Way.

Edwin's, the greengrocer's, have occupied these premises for many years, but such shopkeepers have been increasingly threatened by development schemes and uncertainties over planning. A recent check revealed that there was a 27 per cent. decline in the numbers of greengrocers' and fruiterers' in business in the ten year period, 1961–71.

36. KING'S ROAD, CHELSEA, SW3.

This road takes its name from the route covered by Charles II when moving from one palace to another: from St James's to Hampton Court, but from the Sloane Square area westwards to the World's End it is a chaotic muddle of shops mostly, and all of them vieing madly with one another to attract attention. At week-ends dozens of youngsters converge on the place and wander aimlessly from one coffee-bar to another, and tourists are even whisked through the King's Road to get a sampling of the 'young London scene', or whatever is the latest twee phrase of the fashion writers.

Fun for the visitors, maybe, but Chelsea residents find it all a shade wearing.

37. BEDFORDBURY, WC2.

Believe it or not, this emporium, specialising in the type of clothes in which granny, giving Ruth Chatterton and the like something to worry about, created a sensation and brought lumps to the throats of the Ronald Colmans of Surbiton, is to be found only five minutes' walk away from Moss Bros., in Bedford Street, Strand. At the other end of Bedfordbury stage-hands seem to be continuously moving scenery in and out at the stage-door end of the Coloseum.

38. BARNES HIGH STREET, SW13.

The name 'Barnes' probably derives from the Anglo-Saxon word *bern*, signifying a place for storing, or corner. The area is on a corner of land formed by one of those characteristically abrupt bends in the River Thames. The London Postal List gives us some forty-five High Streets in London, and a dozen High Roads. These are normally very old highways and quite likely can be traced back to Roman roads, raised above ground level.

Barnes itself is a pleasant South London suburb, within reasonably quick distance of town yet with a quiet, relaxed style of its own, as is nicely reflected in the etching, a large common nearby and the pleasures of Richmond Park and the river close at hand for the week-ends.

39. PORTSMOUTH STREET, WC2 — THE OLD CURIOSITY SHOP.

One can go on until one is black and blue in the face explaining that if one takes the trouble to read the last chapter of Dicken's famous novel it is explained there that the shop had long ago been pulled down and a fine broad road was in its place, and that the generally accepted view is that it was in Green Street, off Leicester Square. But, not to worry. It *is* a fine old building in Portsmouth Street and if people will persist in regarding this as the original of *The Old Curiosity Shop* in the teeth of evidence drawn from the novel itself that it is not, there seems little point in banging on about it.

After a few brandies George IV quite convinced himself he had been present at the Battle of Waterloo. He often said so, and maybe convinced himself at times that he had been there. When he appealed to Wellington himself the Duke would diplomatically reply: 'I have often heard your Majesty say so.' A like course is recommended whenever discussion about the Old Curiosity Shop tends to get difficult.

40. THE LAMB AND FLAG, ROSE STREET, WC2.

Among the many events associated with this old house is that which became known as the 'Rose Alley Ambuscade' of 1679. Shades of Stanley Weyman! Hard by the tavern John Dryden (1631–1700) was almost done to death by cudgel-men hired by the Duchess of Portsmouth (Louise de Keroualle), one of Charles II's mistresses. She held him responsible for certain scurrilous verses about her then being diligently circulated.

This 'dastardly Attempt on his Life (mercifully perserv'd)' was commemorated each 19 December when the landlord dispensed a Glass of Sack, Posset or Mull'd Ale to all present without Charge. This was called'd DRYDEN NIGHT, and all interested Persons are requested to inquire for an Invitation.'

From this *polite intelligence* you will gather that this is no ordinary house, and you would be right. And, Bernard Nelson Bessunger Esq, is no ordinary landlord. He has been an author, farmer and wine-merchant in his time, and to ensure against his getting bored he has condescended to preside over the proceedings in this tavern for some years now. The fine collection of unusual paintings, framed prints, squibs and pasquinades which embellish the tavern's walls reflect his recondite, quirky and off beat tastes; and, not content with supplying the publick with food and drink alone he has himself made a notable addition to culinary literature with his *Recipes of Old England: Three Centuries of English Cooking, 1580–1850* (1973).

This consists of extracts directly from original sources, using the archaic spelling and style. Mr Bessunger then recommends his own modifications to make the old recipe practical for the modern cook.

Always a fair sprinkling of 'theatricals' in the bars, which is understandable since lunch-time plays are staged during the week in one of the tavern's large upstairs rooms.

41. YE OLDE COCK TAVERN, FLEET STREET, EC4.

Before you get bemused with tales of the patronage enjoyed in ye olde days and ye olde inn, remember, that none of them were ever in *this* place! The Cock Tavern was moved from the other side of the street in 1887, so it was in the vanished one that Samuel Pepys entertained Mrs Knipp, the noted actress, on the night of 23 April 1668, and to which Tennyson, Dickens, Thackeray, and others resorted.

However, the present place is lively enough and enjoys the faithful patronage of Fleet Street men, lawyers from the Temple, the discriminating London explorer, and the casual tourist. The dining-room there is, naturally known as the Dickens room. What else?

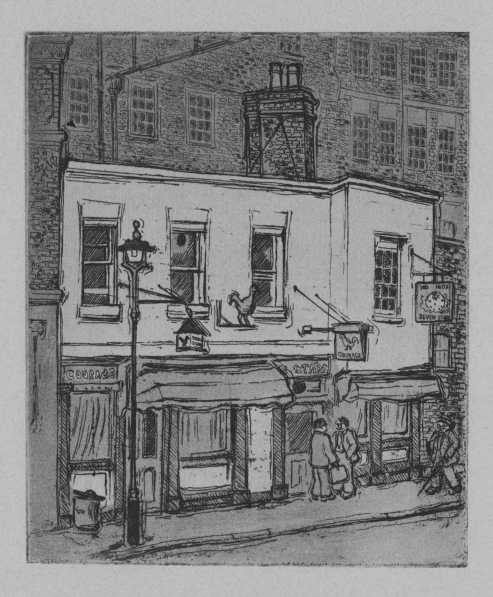

42. SEVEN STARS, CAREY STREET, WC2.

This smallish tavern at the back of the Law Courts in the Strand is little more than a longish room, really, and was known originally as The Leg and Seven Stars. It was named so in honour of the United Provinces of the Netherlands. The building claims to date back to 1602, and it is quite on the cards that this is so as there a number of genuinely old houses in the area. The bars are pleasantly decorated with a mass of framed pictures of Dickensian interest and framed portraits of 'Spy' caricatures of famous judges and counsel of the late nineteenth century.

A few yards away in the same street, but often missed by casual visitors, parish-boundary stones can be seen denoting the boundaries of the two parishes of St Dunstan's-in-the-West, Fleet Street, and St Clement Danes, of 'Oranges and Lemons' fame, in the Strand.

43. YE OLDE WINE SHADES, MARTIN LANE, EC4.

This hostelry has a fine early nineteenth century flavour about it. The impressive front should catch your eye and evoke the inevitable reaction and phrase: 'How Dickensian!' Indeed, the place seems to have sprung straight off the page of a Cruikshank illustration to a Dickens novel. Inside there are stalls, a long bar and agreeable waitresses to attend to your needs.

It is the only other branch of El Vino's (of Fleet Street fame) in London and claims to be the oldest wine-house still operating in the City. Anyhow, this claim came in handy in 1972, when, as a result of a public enquiry, Ye Olde Wine Shades was declared a protected building. Good show! Carry on drinking!

44. THE JAMAICA WINE HOUSE, ST MICHAEL'S ALLEY, EC3.

This place is hard to miss in your City ramblings since it has a large Victorian illuminated sign as well as a blue plaque on the wall proudly proclaiming the fact that it stands on the site of London's first coffee-house, which was opened in 1652 by Daniel Edwards, the City merchant, and his Greek servant, Pasqua Rosee. And, as they do say, *that* started something. Consult Brian Lillywhite's *London Coffee-Houses* (1963) to see how true that statement is, and reflect for a moment on the prominent place the coffee-houses have in eighteenth-century literature and social life.

The interior today is richly panelled, snug and comfortable. The exterior is stone-built.

45. DIRTY DICK'S WINE HOUSE, BISHOPSGATE, EC2.

A visit to this place is almost mandatory whenever the whim takes you to stroll down Petticoat Lane way. The question everyone asks whenever they are taken to this somewhat 'spiky' hostelry is: who was Dirty Dick? The answer is, Nathaniel Bentley, and the story as it has come down to us goes something like this: Bentley's father amassed a considerable fortune, kept a carriage, and maintained a country house, too, which was somewhat unusual for an eighteenth century City tradesman. He also presented a bell to a City church, to be rung on his birthday each year, which custom was kept up until the year of his death, 1761, when he left his extensive property to his son, Nat.

His father, in the manner of many successful business-men, gave his son the advantages he had never had himself: an expensive education, and, even according to some accounts, a sampling of foreign travel (it was the age of the Grand Tour still) to widen his mind. So, the new landlord caused quite a sensation when he took over from his father, with his cultivated speech and manners, his fashionable, dandy-like dress, and his hair arranged and dressed by a court perruquier. This made his subsequent lapse into shabbiness and eccentric scruffiness even more remarked upon than it might otherwise have been in an age by no means short of eccentrics.

The reason for the change is said to have been due to the news being brought him of his bride-to-be's sudden death on the very day arranged for the wedding, and as he was superintending arrangements for a splendid reception of the wedding-guests. In his anguish he ordered the dining-room to be sealed up. It was never reopened in his lifetime, and the lavishly prepared meal was left to the mice, rats, and spiders to nibble their way through. It is a great story, and one wonders if Dickens got the idea of Miss Havisham in *Great Expectations* out of the tale.

46. THE SHIP, LIME STREET, EC3.

This public-house has kept its Victorian character very well; it is full of mirrors, columns, and advertising on glass in pink and gold lettering in which the merits of various brands of drinks, cigars and foods are proclaimed. Much more like the old seafarer's pub in our view than most of the places one sees around in town where the interior decorators have done a half-Nelson on the premises in their desperate efforts to inject a nautical touch.

47. THE GEORGE, STRAND, WC2.

This rambling, old-fashioned tavern has dark pannelling, built-in, bench-style seating and solid four-square tables which positively invite you to stay awhile. The pub's origins can be traced back to 1723, the early Hanoverian period. Arthur Murphy (1727–1805), the Irish dramatist refers to it as the place 'where the town wits met every evening.' These included Goldsmith, who even had his letters addressed to him there. Murphy produced a biography of Dr Johnson before Boswell got round to publishing his. He also stage-managed one of the most important events in Dr Johnson's life: he introduced him to the Thrales.

Naturally, being adjacent to the Middle Temple, and bang opposite the Law Courts the house attracts custom from the lawyers and thereabouts. This includes law students and those, too, from King's College nearby. Usually lively, and especially so at lunchtime on weekdays.

48. YE OLDE CHESHIRE CHEESE, WINE OFFICE COURT, EC4.

If you believe everything they tell you here about Dr Johnson you will leave mildly wondering when this alleged Ale-house Socrates ever found time to write anything, let alone produce his world-famous *Dictionary*. The fact that he was virtually a teetotaller for years at a stretch is blandly disregarded by the tale-spinners. Even the assiduously garnered information in *The Book of the Cheese* (which you can purchase in the house) on the 'Dr Johnson dined here' thesis is terribly slim and unsatisfactory. However, it is a genuinely old house with bags of character and is always a delight to revisit.

The present house was rebuilt just immediately after the Great Fire, in 1667, and if that is not ancient enough for you, *get lost* in the cellars! Ask the waiter when the next batch of visitors are due to be taken around the vaults. These lie beneath the unsuspecting feet of many a patron in the sawdust-strewn bars above at ground level. They are part of the fourteenth-century crypt of the old Carmelite monastery thereabouts. Hence the local placenames: Whitefrairs Street, Carmelite Street, and numerous variants on them. This will really make your visit memorable.

Entre nous, we have a lively suspicion that it was one of the Cheese's most loyal patrons, George Augustus Sala, who foisted the Dr Johnson-Cheshire Cheese legend upon us all. A man who could dream up the 'succulent bivalve' to describe an oyster could fabricate anything.

49. WIG AND PEN CLUB, STRAND, WC2.

The building itself is structurally very interesting since it dates back to 1628 and was the only one in the area to escape damage in the Great Fire (1666). The Club's members are largely drawn from Fleet Street newspapers, the advertising and publishing world, together with a discreet lacing of lawyers and business executives.

The fine display of 'Spy' cartoons in the club's windows and reception-area invariably catch the eye of passers-by. If you have the good fortune to be taken in any time as a guest there are some fine framed prints, many of them of a topographical character of old London, to be seen.

50. YE OLDE DOCTOR BUTLER'S HEAD, MASON'S AVENUE, EC2.

Medicinal ale? Just what the doctor ordered! Quite so! Dr William Butler, Court Physician to James I, is deservedly remembered for his invention of medicinal ale. It became popular in his own day and several houses prospered by selling it. His notions of shock treatment for patients, though, is more open to question. When he had to deal with someone suffering from, or suspected to be suffering from epilepsy he would whip out a brace of loaded pistols he normally kept secreted away in a desk and fire the thing off without warning. That was *his* idea of shock treatment! I have wondered sometimes if it was an addled, fuddled remembrance of this which inspired Jack Mytton's desperate expedient of setting light to his nightshirt to cure the hiccups.

This is an unusual, rambling old-fashioned kind of house, with a first-floor dining-room, much favoured by the staffs of the nearby banking and insurance offices at lunch-time.

51. GEORGE INN, THE BOROUGH HIGH STREET, SEI.

The George stands on the site of a much older inn of the same name, and until the 1880s it was enclosed on three sides of the yard. Local tradition has it that Shakespeare himself acted here, which is quite possible, since his Globe Theatre was close by, and inn courtyards were often requisitioned for 'instant theatre'.

Scenes from his plays are still performed annually, the wooden galleries with their heavy balustrades doing service as ready-made stage sets. Members of the dramatic groups in the Dickens Fellowship also play out scenes from the novels against the same backdrop.

If one takes friends there for the first time, their first words are invariably: 'Straight out of Dickens, isn't it?' And, so it is. In Chapter Ten of *The Pickwick Papers* Dickens describes the Borough's many coaching inns of the 1820s. The literature on them is quite enormous and literary references continuous from the time Chaucer's pilgrims to Canterbury set out from the Tabard Inn, through Shakespeare's plays and beyond to Dickens' time. The railway age was just round the corner when he wrote *Pickwick*, and it was the railways, of course, which gave the old stage-coaches their *quietus*. The George, or what is left of it, is a reminder of the departed glories of the coaching age. Lots of character about The George and the area.

52. THE GUINEA, BRUTON PLACE, W1.

If you happen on this place unawares you may feel like a puppy with two tails, with *your* 'discovery' of a London pub nobody knows – until you get inside! Very popular and crowded, you will find it, and beyond the bar there is an elegant dining-room, and that, too, always appears to be pretty fully booked. In summer-time half the lunch-time bar patrons spill out on to the pavement outside and keep up lively conversations as they drink.

Bruton Place is a tiny, mews-style thoroughfare which runs from the north-east corner of Berkeley Square in an easterly direction. It has an L-shaped kind of ending, which, if you follow round, brings you out into Bruton Street.

53. I AM THE ONLY RUNNING FOOTMAN, HAY'S MEWS, WI.

The tavern's curious name reminds us of that elegant world glimpsed every time we see a modish, well-mounted production of, say, *The School for Scandal* or *The Rivals*, of that glittering *beau-monde* of which Sheridan was himself so dazzling an ornament. Of days when noblemen strutted around like kings themselves, surrounded by an obsequious and numerous court: butlers, personal stewards, footmen, personal chaplains, even who maybe had earlier acted as tutors to them and accompanied them on the Grand Tour. So many noblemen lived thereabouts in the squares, Berkeley Square, Grosvenor Square, and the equally fashionable streets that ran out of them, their servants alone constituted an important part of the local population. Servants had their own 'locals' then, and this was one of them. It had been known earlier as The Running Horse, but the name was changed by the 4th Duke of Queensberry, who died in 1810.

The attractive signboard bears the legend: 'I am the Only Running Footman', and inside the bar itself there is, over the fireplace, a striking modern painting, a kind of historical reconstruction, as it were, of a scene once familiar enough to Londoners about the time Henry Fielding sat as a magistrate at Bow Street and wrote *Tom Jones*. In it we see the carriage of a Man of Quality, obviously, lumbering its hearse-like way through a street, preceded by a running footman in livery, blowing a horn to clear the path for his master. Startled passers-by pause to watch the cavalcade go by, whilst delighted children weave their way in and out of the crowds as they keep pace with the carriage.

54. THE DOVES, UPPER MALL, HAMMERSMITH, W6.

This is a lovely old riverside inn with a roofed verandah and a grape-bearing vine from where privileged spectators can witness the annual Oxford and Cambridge boat race and enjoy their beer at the same time.

When the house was made into two, No. 17 was transformed into what was delightfully termed a 'smoking box' for Queen Victoria's uncle, the Duke of Sussex. There is some dispute over the pub's real name: The Dove, or The Doves. One tale is that it was originally The Dove but was given its plural form by mistake when the place was repainted some time in the past.

Charles II's widow, Catherine of Braganza lived nearby, and a later occupant of the royal widow's home was Dr John Radcliffe of Oxford, his fortune creating the Library, Infirmary and Observatory there named after him.

James Thompson, poet, and author of *The Seasons*, was fond of the view of the river from the tavern's premises and sat gazing reflectively at the water there for hours on end. There is a monument to him in the porch of Richmond Parish Church.

55. WELL'S TAVERN, WELL WALK, HAMPSTEAD, NW3.

Built in the 1830s, the house-name reminds us of the days when Hampstead Wells rivalled those of Tunbridge Wells and Epsom as a spa. Well Walk close by used to be bordered with rows of elms and limes. In the mid-nineteenth century Tennyson's mother spent the last years of her life here.

There is a pleasant, family hotel atmosphere about this house. The restful kind of port of call which is welcome after, say, a nice summer's day visit to Fenton House, Kenwood, and Keat's House, which are all close at hand.

56. THE BLACK FRIAR, QUEEN VICTORIA STREET, EC4.

This curiosity of London publand was designed by H. Fuller Clark in the year of Queen Victoria's Diamond Jubilee (1897), and contains many interesting features, even the exterior being embellished with intricate mosaic work, wrought-iron hanging signs, and copper panels. Its name reminds us of the large thirteenth-century Dominican priory in the area. Inside, a series of panels by Henry Poole R.A., encapsulates some riotously funny but staunch, late-Victorian Protestant notions of what the monastic life was all about. As Ian Nairn says: 'The theme of bibulous friars is flogged to death'; and when they are not drinking they are fishing for next Friday's meatless day meals. Judging by the size of the fish they land they won't fall apart before Saturday! However, as Nairn says: 'When the pressure of friardom lets up the effect is much better and also more Art Nouveau, like the little bar on the corner. But much worth seeing, in any case; there is nothing else like it.' We will all say Amen to that!

72

57. YE OLDE SPOTTED DOG, UPTON LANE, E7.

During an attack of plague in London in 1603 The Spotted Dog was used as an Exchange by City merchants, and again during the Great Plague, 1665–6 the merchants held their Exchange in a room which was commemorated by a painting of the City Arms on a wall.

Upton Lane also claims associations with Dick Turpin, the highwayman, who married a West Ham girl. But, one is wary of regurgitating much of the information blithely decanted in the past from one book to another about Turpin since modern historians have established that much of it 'ain't necessarily so,' as the song has it.

However, another story of a name-dropping character connected with this hostelry has it that Charles II and a party of his followers showed up after hunting at Hornchurch in search of refreshment. As it was late the landlord had already retired to bed, and was none to pleased about being woken up by a noisy crowd, and told 'em, without mincing words, what he thought of 'em! But Charles, being Charles took it all as a huge joke, and when his identity was made known, the landlord, of course was equally profuse in his apologies and bustled around to supply the king and his followers with all they required. In return, Charles II granted him a full licence to keep open day and night. But, what with all the current chatter about working 'unsocial hours' we *do* not recommend that you say too much about *that* to the barman next time you call in at The Spotted Dog!

58. YE OLDE WATLING, BOW LANE, EC4.

This delightful old house on the corner of Bow Lane and Watling Street boasts associations with Sir Christopher Wren, which is not surprising since it lies only a stone's-throw away from his great cathedral. Anyhow, it has what it calls a Wren Bar, among its other attractions, and there are plenty of prints of old London about. There are massive wooden benches, nicely aged, and a curiously cosy, Dickensy atmosphere about the place. A genuine village pub, bang in the heart of the City itself; for years a fine old cat sprawled with Cleopatra-like languor on one of the window-sills and graciously endured endless stroking by delighted patrons.

59. THE GRENADIER, WILTON ROW, SW1.

This amusing hostelry is tucked away in a mews behind Wilton Crescent, and is an ideal port of call after visiting Apsley House since, here too, you are surrounded by a mass of old prints relating to the Duke of Wellington and his officers. A well-attested tradition has it that the premises cover the old billeting headquarters of Wellington's officers. The Old Barrack Yard was close by.

Like so many of the houses featured in this book, The Grenadier, too, retains a nice villagey atmosphere about it, and a fairly faithful set of regulars. These seem to be agreeably young, bright, and lively. The barmen sport regimental white mess jackets and insignia of rank.

60. HOOP AND GRAPES, ALDGATE HIGH STREET, EC3.

By luck this hostelry just missed the Great Fire (1666) by a whisker, by fifty yards to be precise, and much of the inn's original fabric survives. It was a private dwelling, then, although later a vintner took over, which explains the large cellars. One is naturally chary of perpetuating the claim in print, that, as the house itself claims: 'it is the oldest licenced house in London, dating back to the thirteenth century,' but it *is* certainly an old house, and well worth dropping in to see, but *never on Saturdays*.

It has a six-day licence only, and Sunday is a busy day usually, anyhow, as crowds converge on nearby Petticoat Lane (Middlesex Street) to enjoy the unusual spectacle of the Sunday market there.

76

61. THE SUN INN, BARNES, SW13.

This popular house started off life as a coffee-house in the eighteenth century. Local documents mention a blacksmith's shop and three cottages 'situate near the Sun Inn' in 1747. Alterations have occurred, naturally, over the years but we imagine that structurally it retains many of its eighteenth century features. As can be seen from the drawing it is one of those houses that encourages 'extramural students.' In summer-time there are invariably cheerful family groups enjoying themselves at the tables set out for them in the front of the house in an agreeable, civilised way.

62. THE WINDSOR CASTLE, CAMPDEN HILL ROAD, W8.

Built in 1835, this pub at the highest point of Campden Hill Road retains much of the charm of the country tavern, with its alcoved-style, bench-like seats in dark wood, framed John Leech illustrations to Surtees novels, and a view of Windsor Castle, reminding us of the days when it was, indeed, possible from this high vantage point, to get a view of Windsor Castle across the fields. There is a charming garden at the back of the tavern which becomes increasingly popular during the summer months and where chairs and tables are laid out for patrons.

63. THE COCKPIT, ST ANDREW'S HILL, EC4.

This old house, formerly known as The Three Castles, stands on the site of an old cock-fighting pit; and this, naturally, supplies it with a ready-made excuse for its fine collection of cock-fighting prints after Ben Marshall (1768–1835) and others, and evokes memories of that somewhat rough-and-tumble London of Pierce Egan's Tom and Jerry in *Life in London* (1820).

It is a curiously sited building, tall and unusual, and worth looking into after you have been to The Black Friar (see No. 56). It is only five minutes' away.

79

64. MAGPIE AND STUMP, OLD BAILEY, EC4.

Naturally, they would have us believe that this is the Magpie and Stump mentioned in *The Pickwick Papers* although most Dickens scholars incline to the view that this was a 'disguised' name and that the house Dickens had in mind was either the George IV or the Old Black Jack in Portsmouth Street, Lincoln's Inn Fields. Both were demolished in 1896, although the George IV was rebuilt. However, the house does not lack one piece of literary renown about which there can be no argument. The Revd Richard Barham, sometime Canon of St Paul's, has a ghoulish reference in *The Ingoldsby Legends* to Lord Tomnoddy, who, bored with life and seeking diversion of some kind, hired the whole first floor of the Magpie and invited twenty friends along for an all-night drinking session and a grandstand view of a public hanging at Newgate opposite next morning. But they all drank themselves so silly they missed the hanging!

The last time anything like that happened, of course, was on 26 May 1868, when Michael Barratt, a Fenian, was hanged outside Newgate. That was London's last public hanging, and the Central Criminal Court stands now on the site of Newgate Gaol in Old Bailey.

When James I married Anne, daughter of Christian IV, the tavern's name was changed to The King of Denmark and it was many years before it reverted to its old and present title. Naturally, it is a busy house, and an engaging sign showing a magpie perched on the base of an old tree, probably tempts many a passer-by to look in.

65. HAND AND SHEARS, MIDDLE STREET, CLOTH FAIR, EC1.

Not much to look at on the outside, maybe, but this is a house of ancient origin, where the Court of Pie Poudre (i.e. of Dusty Feet) was held in former time to settle disputes arising between citizens at Bartholemew Fair. They granted licences, tested weights and measures to ensure fair trading, and imposed penalties on fraudulent traders.

Although the Lord Mayor himself formally proclaimed the fair open at the Hand and Shears, an informal practice grew up for the fair to be irregularly opened beforehand by a company of tailors who met at the tavern the night before. They elected a chairman, and, as the clock struck midnight issued forth into Cloth Fair, each with a pair of shears in his hand, to give the lively and expectant crowds gathered thereabouts permission to begin their carnival capers. There is a fair-size literature on the fair itself, including a play of Ben Jonson's actually entitled *Bartholemew Fair*. It lasted into the nineteenth century, but increasing protests from City dwellers and traders about the rowdyism it engendered led to its abolition. The best book on the subject remains Henry Morley's old classic, *Memoirs of Bartholemew Fair* (1892). It is still a lively house with a lot of character about it and popular with business-men throughout the day and those connected with Smithfield Market.

66. YE OLDE MITRE TAVERN, ELY COURT, ECI.

This delightful old tavern is tucked away in a small courtway that can be approached two ways: either from Hatton Garden, or from Ely Place itself, where you will find St Etheldreda's, the only pre-Reformation church in the City of London to return to Catholic hands. It has been administered by the Rosminian Fathers since 1873. It once formed part of the medieval palace of the Bishops of Ely. This explains the tavern's origin and name, really, since it was built in 1546 by Bishop Goodrich for his palace servants, and, as the sign in the drawing shows, since it features the bishop's mitre and the date of the tavern's foundation: 1546.

It is a house with a lot of character, atmosphere, tradition, and history, and its bars are all of a snug, intimate kind.

67. HOLE-IN-THE-WALL, MITRE COURT, EC2.

Most people have heard of the old Fleet Prison and the Marshalsea, thanks doubtless to Dickens, but it is surprising how often one leads born Londoners, who feel they know their old town, to this curious little hostelry which also has associations with the bad old days of debtors' gaols. It is to be found in a small court tucked away between Wood Street and Milk Street, off Cheapside. In a cellar annexe in the open square the tavern dispenses only wines and beers. It is all that remains of the Old Wood Street Compter, or debtor's prison.

68. THE SHIP, GATE STREET, WC2.

The Ship was established in 1549, and here we are very much in 'Challoner land'. A little further north, in Old Gloucester Street, you will find a blue plaque marking the house where once lived Dr Richard Challoner (1691–1781), Vicar Apostolic of the London District in the days when the penal laws in operation made it a crime to hear Mass, and an even worse one to be a priest and *say* Mass. Nevertheless, Mass was said in secret at The Ship. A look-out generally warned of imminent raids by government officials, thus, when they entered they saw nothing but a group of people sitting round a table with mugs of beer before them and churchwarden pipes, the priest disappearing into the house itself.

Incidentally, the nearby Catholic Church in Kingsway, St Anselm and St Cecilia is the third in the area, and supersedes the earlier chapels of the Sardinian Embassy in the area, where, being extra-territorial and not subject to the operations of the penal laws, many London Catholics heard Mass in the eighteenth century. The first one was sacked and burnt in the Gordon Riots (1780), and a plate showing what the interior of the later chapel built looked like is to be found in Rowlandson and Pugin's *Microcosm of London* (1808). This also disappeared when Kingsway was planned to be replaced by St Anselm and St Cecilia's.

Masonic lodge meetings were also held in The Ship in the eighteenth century.

69. THE PROSPECT OF WHITBY, WAPPING WALL, EI.

A lively place, especially on a Friday or Saturday night, with its jostling crowds, pop singers gyrating and singing against a background of electric guitars, Hawaiian music, Irish reels, or whatever. But, if you fancy a quieter *ambiance* there is the dining-room upstairs and a small bar, not to mention the balcony where Gustave Doré and Dickens drank in the riverside scene at leisure, as, indeed, so many of us have done since. It is a great favourite with visitors, and most guided London tours include the place on their East End runs. In the Pepys Room there is an interesting picture of Doré, dressed as a docker to avoid recognition, sketching the outside of the *Prospect*.

70. THE ANCHOR, BANKSIDE, SEI.

A typical riverside tavern, this, and rich in literary associations. The house Shakespeare used was destroyed in the Southwark fire of 1676, and the present tavern is of eighteenth century date, built in ti me to be visited by Dr Johnson, who, as the personal friend of Henry Thrale, M.P. for Southwark and, we suspect, his speech-writer also, was often in the area at Thrale's brewery. This was sold after his death by his widow to a Quaker gentleman named Barclay and Thrale's right-hand man of business, Mr Perkins. Hence Barclay, Perkins and Dr Johnson's name on the beer bottles. There's literary fame for you!

A new restaurant was added in 1963, but the old part stays much as it was. From a platform built over the river for the benefit of patrons a fine view of St Paul's and the riverfront can be obtained.

Features worth noting, and they do figure in the drawing, are the cast iron bollards by the pub door. They bear the inscription 'CLINK 1812.' The Clink, like the Marshalsea, was another one of Southwark's prisons. It was burnt down by the Gordon rioters in 1780. Incidentally, it was 'the liberty of the Clink', a right attaching to the nearby London palace of the Bishops of Winchester, which first attracted theatres to Southwark in Shakespeare's time. They felt more free from interference there than in the City.

71. THE MAYFLOWER, ROTHERHITHE STREET, SE16.

This is a pleasant, cosy pub on the 'Surrey side' of the Thames, full of polished wood and glass-windows shaped like port-holes. It is the only public-house we know off hand that holds a licence to sell stamps, and out back you can see the stairs from which the Pilgrim Fathers embarked in 1620 to make history in what were then the American colonies. Not far away in the churchyard lie buried some of the organisers of that expedition.

Rotherhithe Street follows the contours of the river, and in places, is lapped by it. Piers and the gridwork of docks combine to give this part of South London a distinctive, nautical tang.

72. THE LONDON APPRENTICE, ISLEWORTH, MIDDLESEX.

In his delightful book on the Bath Road, *And So to Bath* (1940), Cecil Roberts writes: 'Few artists have been able to resist *The London Apprentice*. It recalls the eighteenth century when the young apprentices of the London Guilds came here by boat to celebrate their feast days and holidays.' The drawing rather proves Mr Robert's point, doesn't it?

    Make a point of looking in next time you visit nearby Syon House. After all that Robert Adam and borrowed splendour from Imperial Rome within the riverside palace of the Duke of Northumberland, you will need something quieter. The *'prentice* comes high on the list of hostelries to revisit when spring arrives and the town-bound Londoner begins to think of places to go to at week-ends. This stretch of the Thames offers many choices of places to visit within easy distance of town: Syon House, Osterley, Ham House, Kew Palace and Gardens, Hampton Court Palace and Gardens, not to mention Windsor Castle itself.

73. THE THAMES AT WESTMINSTER, SWI.

Like the view of St Paul's from The Anchor (No. 70), this view of the Palace of Westminster from the terrace alongside County Hall on the 'Surrey side' of the river is a revelation; it enables us to grasp the sheer sweep of Barrie and Pugin's vision when they rebuilt the old Houses of Parliament after the fire of 1834.

The present Westminster Bridge was opened in 1862, and it was the one before that, opened in 1750, upon which Wordsworth loitered and leaned over before immortalising the view therefrom in his famous poem.

Choose a nice day to view the Palace from across the river and drink in the detail. As Lord Clark say, in *The Gothic Revival* (1964): 'Barry had resolved to carry the medieval style right through the buildings down to the minutest detail; down to the inkstands and umbrella stands'; but in spite of criticism at the time, and since, few would disagree with Lord Clark's conclusion: 'I doubt if the most anti-Goth would exchange our Parliament building for the correct and imposing classical senate houses of the Continent.

74. THE VICTORIA EMBANKMENT, WC2.

The Victoria Embankment is a wide, tree-lined thoroughfare which runs alongside the Thames from Blackfrairs Bridge to Westminster, the river here forming part of that stretch known as the King's Reach. The design for the embankment was by Sir Joseph Bazalgette and was completed in 1870. For the connoisseur of detail this is a walk worth making over and over again, taking in the details of all the monuments in the gardens, the lamp standards as shown in the drawing, Cleopatra's Needle, the Egyptian motifs it inspired on the bench-ends which line the Embankment, and much else.

75. STRAND-ON-THE-GREEN, CHISWICK, W4.

This delightful village-in-town has always been a great favourite with artists, and, understandably so, since, apart from the river itself there are several attractive, well-preserved eighteenth-century houses in the area, including some old fishermen's cottages, skilfully converted. The inevitable pub along this stretch of the river, the Bull's Head, is an eighteenth century painted brick building, well-preserved with two stories and an attic overlooking the Thames, and old tiled roof with two dormers, and a modern ground floor.

Past records show the usual chaotic changes of names down the years: Stronde (1378),Strongreene (1636), Strand Green (1677), Strand-in-the-Green (1705), Strand-Under-Green (1754), Strand on Green (1795), and its present form, Strand-on-the-Green, from 1817 onwards.

76. THE THAMES AT RICHMOND, SURREY.

Richmond Bridge (built 1774–77, and a toll-bridge until 1859) is one of the most attractive of the Thames bridges and seems to have quite fascinated eighteenth and nineteenth century painters to judge from the number of paintings of it which exist. The area has always been popular with Londoners and the first sign of good weather brings them flocking to it at week-ends. There is a link between this Richmond, Surrey, and the one in Yorkshire since it was named after the first Tudor, Henry VII, one of whose titles was the Earl of Richmond (i.e. the Richmond in Yorkshire). Before that it was considered part of Sheen. Remnants of the old palace can be seen along the riverside.

77. THE CUTTY SARK, GREENWICH, SEIO.

The *Cutty Sark*, which stands in a special dry dock at Greenwich is the only fully-rigged survivor of the once proud fleet of tea-clippers who made the 'China run' in the nineteenth century. Just as the railways wrote the stage-coachman's obituary, so the advent of steam meant the end of the tea-clippers, but the legend of their performances lingers and enthralls.

The odd thing here, really, is that the *Cutty Sark*, which was built in 1869 and intended to prove itself as the clipper to beat all clippers did not live up to expectations. Frankly, she was a disappointment on the China run and did much, much better on the wool-run to Australia.

Note in the drawing one special feature of the *Cutty Sark*: the hull rising in a curve upwards, to the high broad counter-like stern. In 1954 the Cutty Sark Preservation Society had the ship brought to Greenwich. Go aboard next time you are in Greenwich and marvel at the intricacies of seamanship in the days of sail. There is a fine array of literature on sale aboard the *Cutty Sark*, too, about the vessel and the phenomenon of the tea-clippers and their China run.

78. ST THOMAS MORE STATUE BESIDE CHELSEA OLD CHURCH, SW3.

Outside Chelsea Old Church there is an impressive bronze statue of St Thomas More (1478–1535), one of Chelsea's favourite past residents. It is the work of L. Cubitt Bevis. On Monday, 21 July 1969 it was unveiled by the Speaker of the House of Commons (Dr Horace King), which was appropriate since More had been Speaker, too, in his day, and in the presence of a truly ecumenical gathering: the Archbishop of Canterbury, the Cardinal Archbishop of Westminster, and the Moderator of the Free Church Federal Council. The sadly damaged and war-blitzed church has itself been beautifully restored and most of its famous monument re-sited within it. Chelsea's own 'Man for all Seasons' would approve the good taste, piety and skill which has informed this restoration.

79. ST ANDREW UNDERSHAFT, LEADENHALL STREET, EC3.

Everywhere you go in the City of London you will spot blue plaques on buildings and walls, and if you take the trouble to stop and see what they are all about the odds are that they record the fact that the spot was once holy ground: a church stood there. Of 120 parish churches within the 'square mile' which were there in the pre-Reformation or pre-Great Fire period only eight of medieval date remain. Wren rebuilt many that were destroyed, of course.

St Andrew Undershaft is one of them and is mentioned in twelfth-century records. Its curious name derives from the tall shaft or maypole, which, up to 1517, was set up outside the church each Mayday and over-topped the church tower itself. It was eventually chopped up and burnt as an object of super-stition. The church as we see was rebuilt between 1520 and 1532. The Tower, seen in the drawing, is fifteenth century below, with fire-door and knocker, and Victorian at the top. The impressive nave ceiling within was rebuilt after the late war (1950) and the old bosses put back, but the aisle roofs are original. The font is by Nicholas Stone (1631), there is a very fine pulpit, and the organ case is by Renatus Harris.

95

80. CHURCH PATH, MORTLAKE, SW14.

The drawing opposite shows the attractive approach to Mortlake Parish Church, which boasts of one of the oldest rings of eight bells in the country. The ring in its present form was completed in 1784 (5 of the bells date from 1694). Mortlake itself became famous throughout the world in the seventeenth century when the tapestry works were set up there in 1617. Dutchmen, skilled in the art and craft of tapestry-making were brought from Holland and settled around the High Street area. Quite a literature has grown up about the Mortlake tapestry works, and examples of work from there are to be seen at Ham House, Richmond, Hampton Court Palace, and in the Victoria and Albert Museum.

96

81. ST PAUL'S CATHEDRAL, EC4.

What *is* there to be said about St Paul's that has not been said already, and doubtless, better? Go in there quietly one weekday and sit through Evensong, absorbing the atmosphere and feel of the place, and, as the choir weaves its rhymic way through psalms, anthems, the Magnificat, the Nunc Dimittis, and the rest, do as Wren himself commands, *circumspice*. Never mind the details for the moment, or the dates, you can check back on them any time.

82. WESTMINSTER CATHEDRAL, SWI.

From the newly-laid out piazza which enables people in Victoria Street to see what they may not have realised was there all the time, there, before their very eyes: the magnificent west or main door of Westminster Cathedral, as here depicted.

The Cathedral is the great achievement of John Francis Bentley, who was chosen as its architect in 1894 by Cardinal Vaughan. The Cardinal felt that Gothic was too fussy, too expensive, and would take far too long to build; he urged Bentley to go to Ravenna, to consider the possibilities of adapting the Byzantine style to the requirements of a colder clime. Get the shell up, interior decoration and detail can wait, and proceed as funds permit. That was Bentley's mandate, and all things and difficulties considered, he did a magnificent job and created a perfect setting for the splendour of the Roman liturgy.

By one of those ironies, of which there are so many in history, Bentley died before his splendid campanile was two-thirds completed, and the first really important pontifical ceremony in the newly-opened Cathedral occurred when prelates converged upon it to take part in the solemn obsequies of the Cardinal whose vision had inspired the building of the new cathedral which would stand comparison with the great ones of the past.

We never catch sight of that campanile on the skyline, challenging the indifference and materialism of the age without thinking of the choir within thundering out that triumphant versicle from the Psalms: *nequando dicant gentes, Ubi est Deo eorum*: unless the Gentiles should say: Where is thy God? Westminster Cathedral is the answer Bentley and Cardinal Vaughan have given us.

83. DEAN'S YARD, WESTMINSTER, SW1.

The Deanery stands where once the medieval abbots' house did and in a quiet square within the shadow of both the Abbey itself and Westminster School. There is a leisurely Barchester-like calm about the area which is in marked contrast to the bustle at the Abbey's main, west-door where batches of camera-slung tourists battle their way into the Abbey at the same time as other tourists, equally determined, try to get out.

84. WESTMINSTER ABBEY, SWI.

The history of the Abbey is very much that of the nation itself since our sovereigns have been crowned here since the time of William of Normandy (1066). Many famous people lie buried in the Abbey and many more commemorated either by a monument, brass or tablet. Dickens is buried in Poet's Corner, for example, but his great contemporary, Thackeray, is only commemorated there, in a bust by his friend, Baron Marochetti. His mortal remains rest at Kensal Green cemetery. Chaucer, Dryden, Edmund Spencer, Ben Jonson, Samuel Johnson, David Garrick; yes, these are buried within. And, beyond Poets' Corner lie the royal tombs.

As the Abbey stands now it is substantially as it was rebuilt in the fourteenth century by Henry III. He was much impressed by the achievements of the great French cathedral builders of his day and the rebuilt Abbey reflects his distinctive French taste. In a sense he saw the Abbey like a monstrance with the tomb of St Edward the Confessor, like the Host at its centre, and everything else in the Abbey radiating from it. Near the Confessor lie those kings whom Shakespeare wrote about in his historical plays: Richard II and his Queen; Henry V of Agincourt. Further eastwards lies the splendour of the Henry VII Chapel, inviting comparison with St George's Chapel, Windsor, and masses of tombs and commemorative monuments in all the various side-chapels. Once again, as in St Paul's, take time out to sit through Choral Evensong, absorb something of the spirit and *ethos* of this sacred place, and feel the place come alive as the choristers' voices pierce the air. Detailed study of the inscriptions on tombs, checking dates and the names of sculptors can wait for a rainy day and the library.

85. WESTMINSTER ABBEY — SIDE VIEW.

A sideview of the main entrance to Westminster Abbey, showing the pathway which leads to the North
Door entrance which takes you directly into the Statesmen's Aisle. Once again, as regards monuments:
Gladstone is both buried here and has a monument; Disraeli has a monument, true, but he is buried at
the parish church besides his beloved Hughenden Manor, in Buckinghamshire.

And, within a stone's-throw of the North Door there is St Margaret's, Westminster, 'Parish Church
of the House of Commons'. It has a special interest for Americans since Sir Walter Raleigh, the founder
of Virginia, who was beheaded in Old Palace Yard in 1618, is buried in the chancel, and, indeed, it has a
number of other American associations of an interesting kind.

86. HORSE GUARDS WHITEHALL, SW1.

The old stone building you see in the drawing dates from 1758 and stands on the site of the tiltyard of Westminster, so renowned in the courtly annals of jousts and life in Tudor high society. If you pass through the archway in the picture you come out on to the Horse Guards Parade where the annual ceremony of the Trooping of the Colours is staged in celebration of the birthday of H.M. the Queen, who, superb horsewoman as she is, usually steals the show from the soldiers every year. And, beyond, lies St James's Park.

The Horse Guards is the headquarters of the Army London District and is always sentinelled by impressively-dressed and accoutred Household Cavalrymen, whose appearance, as Nance Fyson reveals with quiet wit, strike the admiring gaggle of children below one of them dumb – well, at least for a second or so!

Connoisseurs of military ceremonial are very much in luck in this area since there is always something going on, or in rehearsal. Changing of the Guard? Which one? The one at Buckingham Palace (where Christopher Robin went with Alice) is a foot-guard, but in Whitehall we have the Horse Guards, and quite often the relieving guard will come down from Knightsbridge Barracks and Constitution Hill on their way to Whitehall, and when they do, or the returning guard is doing the same journey in reverse, those who wait to see the guard-change at Buckingham Palace catch elements of both guard-changes and spectacles. The Whitehall 'change' usually takes place on weekdays at 11am (10am or thereabouts, Sundays), and there is a guard-inspection at 4pm.

As is normal on all military guard duty, the men do one hour on before they are relieved, so, maybe the guard who is being gawped at and commented upon by cheeky children in the drawing is consoling himself with the thought that he has only another ten minutes to go!

87. GUILDHALL, EC2.

In 1411 Robert Fabyan, Alderman of the City of London, reported that 'the Guylde Hall of London began to be new-edyfied and of an olde and lytell Cottage made into a fayre and goodly house.' A chapel adjoining the hall was dedicated on 30 October 1444 and improvements of one kind and another continued to be made until 1501 when the hall was reckoned to be complete. This was the Guildhall which suffered such grievous damage in the Great Fire (1666). The Hall, as reconstituted after the Fire, continued in use until 1862 when the Court of Common Council resolved that the flat roof should be replaced by an open roof conforming to the medieval architecture of the building. This Victorian roof was burnt in the blitz in the Second World War and much refurbishing and rebuilding has been done since to get the old Guildhall back into commission. You will find all that heavy early nineteenth-century sculpture is back *in situ*, Nelson, the elder Pitt *et al.*, whilst Gog and Magog preside still over civic functions, meetings, and dinners – but they are *novi homines*, of course, since our former giant protectors were war-time casualities. They had to be replaced after the war by new models fashioned by James Woodforde in the style of Cibber's originals.

The odd thing is that in spite of the historical record of all these changes and disasters which have befallen it the Guildhall somehow looks much as everyone remembers it.

103

88. THE TOWER OF LONDON, EC3.

The Tower of London, which is just outside the City boundaries ('on the outside, looking in') covers about 18 acres. The original Tower, 'The White Tower', was built by William the Conqueror for the double-purpose of protecting and controlling the City, but examples of the architectural styles of all periods can be found somewhere within the Tower, which has sired a whole series of towers-within-the-Tower, and of varying dates and purposes.

The Great or White Tower contains a staggeringly rich collection of armour and weapons, some of it worn by past sovereigns, and is visited by scholars and experts from all parts of the world. The armour and the Crown Jewels are the main attractions for the visitors who literally pour into the place during the summer months.

Technically, it is like Windsor Castle, a royal palace although royalty have not lived in the Tower since Charles II's time. And, like Windsor, although the Tower has plenty of medieval history to its credit, the buildings themselves are often, we feel, more Walter Scott than Froissart; that is, here as at Windsor, there has been a lot of of heavy-handed nineteenth-century restoration-work done. There are glossy books galore about the Tower but the best moneysworth remains the official H.M.S.O. publications sold on the premises.

Tower Bridge, which was opened in 1894 by the City Corporation at the cost of over a million pounds, is a fascinating addition to the London skyline: a late Victorian dream of engineering which has long given delight to schoolboys and provided Sir John Betjeman with something to write about.

89. THE BRITISH MUSEUM, GREAT RUSSELL STREET, WCI.

The British Museum, which was founded in 1753 from the collections of Sir Hans Sloane and Sir Robert Cotton, and has grown, like Topsy, ever since, gathering fresh treasures constantly. In the early nineteenth century the old British Museum was in a state of advanced decay, the collections were endangered, and the construction of a new building had become an urgent necessity. Following an initial grant of £40,000 by the House of Commons towards the expenses, Robert Smirke was commissioned to design the present building, as seen in the accompanying drawing.

Begun in 1827, work on the building went on slowly, but with the erection of the railings along Great Russell Street in the summer of 1852, Smirke's task may be deemed to have been complete. Now, as we go to press, work has begun on the cleaning of the front elevation of the museum: the first time it has been done since the building was completed. The museum authorities state that they hope the cleaning of the facade of the British Museum will restore the building to its fine original appearance, which was intended to be in the words of a contemporary: 'chaste and grand and truly classical.'

90. TRAFALGAR SQUARE, SWI.

This drawing of Trafalgar Square takes in one of Sir Edwin Landseer's lions at the base of Nelson's Column, and gives us a clear view of the National Gallery, designed by William Wilkins (1832–38). One curious feature here: the portico is a 'transplant' from the Prince Regent's demolished residence, Carlton House. The drawing gently underlines the fact that for many Londoners and visitors alike Trafalgar Square has a strange fascination: an oasis of leisure amidst the swirl and roar of mid-town traffic.

91. HER MAJESTY'S THEATRE, HAYMARKET, SWI.

From the National Gallery we move to the theatre which saw productions mounted with such splendour by Sir Herbert Beerbohm Tree in his heyday, that someone said he had transformed Her Majesty's into the National Gallery of the Theatre. Tree opened His Majesty's Theatre in style on the night of 28 April 1897, the year of Queen Victoria's Diamond Jubilee, and it was named in her honour, naturally. He almost lived in the dome of 'my beautiful theatre' for years dreaming up endless ideas for new and spectacular productions. He became one of the early actor-knights and founded the Royal Academy of Dramatic Art.

Her Majesty's stands on a site which had long-standing theatrical connections. There had been a theatre there since 1705; the one Vanbrugh built.

92. THE THEATRE ROYAL, DRURY LANE, CATHERINE STREET, WC2.

The theatre can trace its pedigree back to 1663 when Charles II gave his well-beloved friend Thomas Killigrew a royal charter or patent to establish a theatre for his own company of players. The present building, seen in the drawing opposite, dates from 1812, and in these post-war years has seen a dazzling succession of musical comedy hits: *My Fair Lady*, *Oklahoma!*, *Carousel*, *South Pacific*, *The King and I*, and *A Chorus Line*.

93. HYDE PARK, W1.

Cooped up in town? Hyde Park covers 361 acres and spills over into Kensington Gardens (275 acres), so, bang in the centre of town Londoners have plenty of open space. Henry VIII used it as a deer-park; the Stuarts staged horse-racing in it; George II's consort, Queen Caroline of Anspach, created one of the park's most attractive features, the Serpentine. Here we see some appreciative people making good use of their leisure and the park.

94. ST JAMES'S PARK, SW1.

Another royal park (93 acres, this time). Charles II employed Le Nôtre, the famous French gardener to transform it from a deer-park into a garden. From the bridge, which would be in view of the deck-chair idlers depicted here, there can be obtained one of the most enchanting views in London.

95. HAMPSTEAD HEATH, NW3.

Hampstead Heath, with West Heath and Hampstead Heath Extension thrown in, covers 320 acres, and to the west you have Golders Hill (36 acres), not to mention Parliament Hill Fields (270 acres) to the south-west, and then there is Kenwood (210 acres), with the Iveagh Bequest. Thus Hampstead residents have the advantage of easy access to the town combined with the freedom of one of the most pleasant and exciting of London's open spaces, all on their doorstep. Constable painted many views of the Heath in his Hampstead years, and, indeed, it is unusual to cross the Heath at any time without spotting at least one or two people out sketching or painting. From Hampstead's heights one gets some marvellous panoramic views of the town.

96. STAPLE INN, WC1.

Opposite Gray's Inn Road are some of the oldest houses in London, dating from the Elizabethan period, though they did undergo a complete renovation a few years ago. Their projecting timbered fronts form the street side of Staple Inn which you get to through an archway between the shops. This old Chancery Inn contains two courtyards in which Mr Snagsby liked to walk in summer time and observe how countrified the sparrows and leaves to be found there were. *Bleak House*, this. Then there is Mr Grewgious of the *Mystery of Edwin Drood*, who lived in a house in the second quadrangle, and in real life Dr Johnson lived there in 1759 and wrote *Rasselas, Prince of Abbysinia*. But let's have Mr Dickens again: 'Staple Inn is one of those nooks the turning into which from the dashing street imparts to the relieved pedestrian the sensation of having put cotton wool in his ears, and velvet soles on his boots.' Maybe so, but a flying bomb in 1944 disturbed the peace of the old place rather sadly. The new Hall, rebuilt in its original style and occupied by the Institute of Actuaries, incorporates material from the bombed building, and altogether the restoration of the surrounding chambers has done much to preserve its old character. In spite of its long association with the law the inn owes its name to an earlier use, to a time when there was a custom house thereabouts where wool was weighed and dues upon it collected.

97. BLOOMSBURY SQUARE, WC1.

This was the first open space to become known as a square and it developed into a fashionable quarter in the eighteenth century. A car-park lies hidden beneath the gardens depicted here: one of many such open spaces dotted about London. Old prints of the area show that at one time the entire north side of the square was occupied by Bedford House, the Duke of Bedford's town house, the gardens of which ran down at the back and to the north into what is now Russell Square.

98. MILBOURNE HOUSE, BARNES, SW13.

There has been a Milbourne House facing Barnes Pond on the west side since the fourteenth century, though it has doubtless been rebuilt at various times. Squire William Milbourne's family lived in the house for several generations. Early in the eighteenth century Henry Fielding, the author of *Tom Jones*, lived there.

Since Barn Elms has disappeared Milbourne House can claim to be the oldest house in the district.

99. PAULTONS SQUARE, CHELSEA, SW3.

One of Chelsea's loveliest squares, it takes its name from Sir Hans Sloane's son-in-law, George Stanley of Paultons, in Hampshire. The houses in it are mostly late Georgian, and date from the 1830s.

100. KENSINGTONS SQUARE, W8.

Building of the square began in James II's reign but it was William III and Mary II who helped make it fashionable when they settled in Kensington Palace in 1689. There followed with them, naturally, the vast train of courtiers, fashionable tradesmen and noblemen attached to the royal service and they began looking for accomodation in the area. This helped Kensington to develop into what the old local histories fondly term 'the old Court suburb.' Many courtiers settled in Kensington Square which still retains something of a courtly air and grace about it. Queen Anne and the first two Georges continued to reside at Kensington but George III cared for neither Kensington nor Hampton Court Palace, both greatly favoured by William III, and since his reign lasted from 1760 to 1820, his neglect of them seems to have set a precedent as no sovereign since has lived in either palaces.

However, from the presence of blue plaques all over the place in the square it is clear that the rising professional classes of the nineteenth century developed a liking for living there. From these we gather that past residents have included both John Stuart Mill and Mrs Patrick Campbell. And, of course, just off the square, in Young Street, Thackeray lived for a time and there wrote *Vanity Fair*.

101. OLD PALACE LANE, RICHMOND, SURREY.

Old Palace Lane is situated near the site of the old Palace of Sheen, first occupied by Henry I in 1125. The palace was rebuilt and restyled Richmond Palace by the first Tudor, Henry VII, in remembrance of his own title as Earl of Richmond (Yorks). By the mid-seventeenth century Richmond Palace had become more or less derelict and only the gateway survives today as a reminder of its past grandeur.

The lane itself was a difficult path. A Local Act of Parliament (1785) included a charge that the lane was to be 'well and sufficiently amended and made commodious'. The White Swan tavern dates from the sixteenth century and the terrace of small, Regency-style houses alongside it were built about 1810.

117

102. THE PARAGON, BLACKHEATH, SE3.

This remarkable piece of property development – seven identical four-storey units, linked by colonnades, facing the heath, is not the work of a fashionable architect but of Michael Searle, an estate surveyor operating in the area around 1792. They suffered damage during the Second World War but have been well restored since by C. Bernard Brown.

Blackheath (267 acres) adjoins Greenwich Park. It is an attractive residential area in which there are a number of interesting period houses well worth looking at.

103. LITTLE VENICE, W2.

In his early nineteenth-century plans for the Prince Regent's private park at Marylebone, and the garden city he proposed creating thereabouts, John Nash suggested that a canal should run through what has since become Regent's Park and link up with the already established Paddington Basin to provide his royal master's ornamental lakes with water and supply a *picturesque* note to the landscape (it was the age of Humphrey Repton, remember).

With the Prince's approval Nash went ahead and formed a company to promote the cutting of the canal. After long drawn out and frustrating setbacks, from which Nash suffered a very severe financial loss, the canal *was* at last opened in 1820. For a detailed account of all this consult Herbert Spencer's *London's Canal* (1961).

The Regent's Canal was intended to join the docks at Limehouse with a branch of the Grand Junction Canal at Paddington. It was over eight miles long and work on it began in 1812. Progress, if it can be called that, went on at the rate of roughly a mile a year, and it was estimated that it would cost £60,000. But, like all such estimates, this one, too, proved wildly optimistic, being 'exceedingly swelled by the extravagant price of which the land required has been obliged to be purchased.'

However, a trip on *Jason*, from opposite 60 Blomfield Road, W9, ('Little Venice') to the London Zoo, and back again if you choose, after your visit to the Zoo, will give you some idea of what Nash had it in mind to do originally, and give you glimpses of parts of London you hardly knew were there.

119

SOME SUGGESTIONS FOR FURTHER READING

COMPILE A LONDON BIBLIOGRAPHY? You must be joking! Indeed, Christopher Hibbert asserts in *London: The Biography of a City* (1977), that there is not, *nor could there ever be*, a comprehensive bibliography of London. In support of this statement he reminds us that in the London Library alone there are well over 200 feet of shelves devoted to the history and topography of London. Thus, to cover ourselves before *we* attempt the impossible, we apologise in advance if we have missed mentioning your favourite London books in this list.

No, what we have attempted to do here is simply mention some books we have found helpful and hope they prove equally so to others. Many of them, in turn, contain bibliographies: an important feature, details about which are included in a number of the entries below.

The solution is that serious students should set about building up their own bibliographies, scaffolding their entries around their own personal London interests, *viz*: Roman London (including news of the latest archaeological finds); Pre-Reformation churches and monasteries; Streets and buildings haunted by Dickens' characters, or personally associated with the great novelist; Wren churches; Theatres, linking up information on them with details about the homes and haunts of famous players; specific areas; transport in London (including railways): a vast and popular field in itself, this; the *moist* and congenial subject of old London taverns and pubs; London's clubland – the list, and the infinite permutations on it are endless.

One suggestion here: decide what *your* special London interests are and start building your own, maybe, highly personal and idiosyncratic book lists. Do so, if you like, as they do in libraries on a card-index system. Personally, I prefer looseleaf binders, such as can be purchased in any stationers', together with pads of punch-holed and lined stationery. These allow more space for extracts to be made from the books listed, and personal comments to be included to remind you of the books' value and relevance to *your* studies. And, if these tend to crowd the page? Not to worry. Run over on to a fresh page, and, indeed on to as many extra pages as you choose. Arrange such folders, subject-wise, and label on the outside for quick reference. That is the beauty of London studies; they offer such a wide choice of themes and areas to work on.

Incidentally, they can be highly recommended to retired folk. Even if they are short of money *they have all the time in the world* (lucky people!) to read their heads off in the local history rooms of their nearest public libraries, and, by making good use of the cheap-fare facilities provided on public transport for senior citizens, they can do a lot of London exploring on a relatively slim budget. They need never be bored. Moreover, in museums and galleries, they never found much time to visit in their busy, workaday lives, maybe, there are continuous lecture-programmes (free), which should help them agreeably to develop fresh interests. Free leaflets giving details of these are usually to be found lying about inside the entrances to these buildings.

Coming back to Christopher Hibbert's remarks: I recall hearing a sad-comic tale related once about an earnest Victorian scholar who resolved to bring out *the* book of books on some subject or other which would make most of his colleagues and rivals look pretty silly. He beavered away like crazy in libraries and muniment-rooms for years, and then, disconcertingly stumbled on the fact that some of the best things on his subject were appearing in a foreign language he did not know. So, he broke off his research, *pro tem*, to master that foreign tongue and so read up this fresh material. He did so. Success! But, alas!, much of the information on which his arguments and conclusions rested was out of date by the time *his* book, *the* book, appeared!

So, forwarned, here goes! Emboldened by the thought that even after making his observations Christopher Hibbert gives us a bibliography, we too, likewise tempt the gods and proffer, for what it is worth, our own list.

All titles were published in London unless otherwise noted.

ACRES, W. M. *The Bank of England from Within, 1694–1900.* 1931. The standard work on the domestic and topographical history of the Bank as a City institution.

ADLER, E. N. *London.* Jewish Communities Series: Jewish Publication Society of America, Philadelphia, 1930.
A good history of the Jewish community in London from the earliest days.

ASH, B. *The Golden City: London Between the Fires 1666–1941.* 1964.
A popular, well-illustrated account aimed at the general reader, but sound and reliable.

BAKER, T. *Medieval London.* 1970.

BANKS, F. R. *London.* Penguin Guides, 1971.
With maps and plans this admirable little pocket guide will help visitors getting around town.

BARKER, T. C. AND ROBBINS, R. M. *A History of London Transport.* 2 volumes, 1963, 1976.
The first volume deals with the nineteenth century and the second volume with the present century. A definitive history and quite indispensable.

BARLEY, M. W. *A Guide to British Topographical Collections.* Council of British Archaeology, 1974.
Covers England, Scotland and Wales by Counties; but invaluable for London, see, especially, pages 53–87.

BARNES, R. M. *The Soldiers of London.* 1963.
A history of London-based regiments from 1550 to 1961.

BARRAT, THOMAS J. *The Annals of Hampstead.* 3 volumes, 1912.
Over 500 illustrations, many of them attractive line drawings in the text.

BARTON, N. J. *The Lost Rivers of London.* 1962.
A very readable survey of London's rivers and streams, most of them now buried below ground in pipes. With a detailed map and many illustrations.

BAYNE-POWELL, ROSOMOND. *Eighteenth-Century London Life.* 1937.

BEAVEN, A. B. *The Alderman of the City of London.* 2 volumes, 1908–13.
A list compiled from the records of the City's aldermen, arranged chronologically and by wards from Henry III's reign to 1912, together with much information as to the status and duties of the aldermen. With biographical notes.

BEDFORD, JOHN. *London's Burning.* 1966.
A beautifully illustrated study of the Great Fire of 1666.

BELL, W. G. *The Great Plague of London in 1665.* 1951.
The Great Fire of London in 1666. 1951.
Based mainly on contemporary accounts, these reprints remain key books on the subjects. Both are illustrated and contain valuable bibliographies.
Fleet Street in Seven Centuries: being a History of the Growth of London beyond the Walls into the Western Liberty, and of Fleet Street to this century. 1912.
A sound, detailed history and invaluable for the area concerned.

BELL, W. G., COTTRILL, F. AND SPON, C. *London Wall Through Eighteen Centuries.* 1937.

BERNSTEIN, HENRY T. 'The Mysterious Disappearance of Edwardian London Fog,' in *The London Journal,* Vol 1, No. 2, 1975.
This article is included here for the benefit of *Bleak House* and Sherlock Holmes addicts who are frequently wondering about the fog that we read about but rarely experience nowadays.

BESANT, SIR WALTER. *The Survey of London.* 8 volumes, 1903–10.
Most good reference sections in London libraries keep a set of these quarto-sized volumes which are copiously illustrated and still worth consulting. Individual titles are as follows: *Early London; Medieval London,* 2 volumes; *London in the Time of the Tudors; London in the Time of the Stuarts; London in the 18th Century; London in the 19th Century; London North of the Thames; London South of the Thames; London City.*

BETJEMAN, SIR JOHN. *Victorian and Edwardian London from Old Photographs.* 1969.
Introduction, picture-captioning and commentary by the Poet Laureate, whose occasional writings on architectural themes are always 'good value'. See especially, Sir John's *First and Last Loves* (1969) for his essays on 'London Railway Stations', 'Nonconformist Architecture', and 'Victorian Architecture'.

BIRD, RUTH. *The Turbulent London of Richard II.* 1949.

BIRKENHEAD, SHEILA. *Peace in Piccadilly: The Story of Albany.* 1958.

BLACKHAM, R. J. *London: For Ever the Sovereign City.* 1932.
A popular account of the constitution and activities of the City Corporation.
The Soul of the City: London's Livery Companies. 1931.
Wig and Gown: The Story of the Temple, Gray's and Lincoln's Inn. 1932.
Covers the literary as well as the legal associations of the Inns of Court. Useful bibliography.

BLACKSTONE, G. V. *A History of the British Fire Service.* 1957.
General in scope, but it does cover London fire services from the earliest times. Illustrated.

BLOOM, J. H. AND JAMES, R. R. *Medical Practitioners in the Diocese of London, 1529–1725.* 1935.

BONE, JAMES. *The London Perambulator*. 1926.
An artist's impressions of London. The illustrations have acquired a pleasant period flavour since the book's publication.

BOOTH, CHARLES (editor). *The Life and Labour of the People in London*. 1902–3.
Booth was one of the earliest of what we now call social scientists. His work is almost a continuation of Henry Mayhew's.

BORER, MARY CATHCART. *Two Villages: The Story of Chelsea and Kensington*. 1973.

BOSWELL, JAMES. *Boswell's London Journal 1762–63*. Edited by Frederick A. Pottle. 1950.
Boswell's Life of Dr Samuel Johnson. Many editions.

BOULTON, W. B. *The Amusements of Old London*. 2 volumes, 1901.

BOYS, THOMAS SHOTTER. *Original Views of London, 1842*. With descriptive notes and an Introduction by E. Beresford Chancellor. 1926.
A reissue of a set of topographical drawings important for the accuracy of their architectural detail, and as a faithful picture of London streets in the early Victorian period. For further information about this great artist see James Roundell's *Thomas Shotter Boys*, 1974.

BRAYBOOK, NEVILLE. *London Green: The Story of Kensington Gardens, Hyde Park, Green Park, and St James's Park*. 1957.

BRETT-JAMES, NORMAN G. *The Growth of Stuart London*. 1935.
A history of the city's *physical* growth in the seventeen century, based on primary sources; there is a very useful annotated bibliography. Highly recommended to lovers of Pepys' and Evelyn's diaries, and to students of Wren's London.

BRIGGS, ASA. *Victorian Cities*. 1967.
Despite Warden Sparrow's insistence that the author's name is an anagram of 'Sir Gas Bag', this study is an important, if sometimes dull work.

BRIGGS, MARTIN S. *Wren the Incomparable*. 1953.

BRITTON, J. AND PUGIN, A. C. *Illustrations of the Public Buildings in London*. 1825.
A magnificent record, with engraved steel plans, elevations and perspectives, of London buildings as, say, the young Charles Dickens would have known them.

BURKE, THOMAS. *The Streets of London Through the Centuries*. 1949.
The distillation of a lifetime's reading by a well-known London writer.

CARPENTER, EDWARD (editor). *A House of Kings: The History of Westminster Abbey*. 1966.

CHAMBERS, R. W. AND DAUNT, M. *A Book of London English, 1384–1425*. 1931.
A collection of extracts from contemporary official records of the City, livery companies'

documents, and wills. Chosen to illustrate English as it was at the time of Chaucer.

CHANCELLOR, E. BERESFORD. *History of the Squares of London*. 1907.
Private Palaces of London. 1908.
The Annals of Fleet Street. 1912.
The Eighteenth Century in London. 1920.
The London of Charles Dickens. 1924.
The Pleasure Haunts of London. 1925.
Lost London. 1926.
The West End, Yesterday and Today. 1926.
The London of Thackeray. 1928.
London Recalled. 1937.
Like Charles G. Harper and others of his day, 'E. B.' was a most assiduous *book-maker*, but his contributions to London literature have a pleasing, relaxed Edwardian charm and are still worth studying for fundamental historical facts.

CHANDLER, T. J. *The Climate of London*. 1965.
A detailed, scientific study with maps, charts and tables. So, if you *must* talk about the weather in town, read this first and talk *knowledgeably*! Lace up, too, with J. H. Brazell's *London Weather*, 1968, a statistical survey of London's changing weather from 1841 onwards, with notes also on outstanding metereological events of earlier days.

CHURCH, RICHARD. *The Royal Parks of London*. 1956.

CLARKE, F. L. *Parish Churches of London*. 1966.

CLUNN, HAROLD P. *The Face of London*. 1970.
A great favourite amongst books on London since it was first published in the 1930s. Reprinted several times. This new edition by E. R. Wetherset has some fine photographic illustrations.

COBB, GERALD. *London City Churches: A Brief Guide*. 1971.
Useful to have in the pocket on quiet rambles and church-visiting forays around the square-mile of the City. Illustrated.
The Old Churches of London. 1948.

COOK, G. H. *Old St Paul's*. 1955.
If you want to know what St Paul's was like *before* it was rebuilt by Sir Christopher Wren this is the book for you. Written by an acclaimed authority on ecclesiastical architecture.

COURSE, EDWIN. *London Railways*. 1962.
An illustrated history and geography of the railways above ground.

CRAIG, SIR JOHN. *The Mint: A History of the London Mint from AD287 to 1948*. 1953.

CREW, A. *The Old Bailey*. 1933.
A London barrister's account of the history and procedure at the Central Criminal Court. Good on notable trials since 1907. Bibliography.

DARK, SIDNEY. *London*. 1924.
An attractive book illustrated by Joseph Pennell.

DARLINGTON, IDA AND HOWGEGO, JAMES. *Printed Maps of London c. 1553–1830*. 1964.
A complete bibliography of London maps, arranged chronologically with notes and locations. A standard work.

DAVIES, G. S. *Charterhouse in London: Monastery, Mansion, Hospital, School*. 1921.
A comprehensive history.

DAVIS, DOROTHY. *A History of Shopping*. 1966.
Covers the subject from medieval days until 1966. With much of value for the London historian.

DAY, J. R. *The Story of London's Underground*. 1972.
One of the best recent short histories.

DE MARE, ERIC. *London's Riverside: Past, Present and Future*. 1958.
Handsomely illustrated with the author's own photographs.

DESANT, A. T. *The History of St James's Square*. 1895.
Piccadilly in Three Centuries. 1914.
Grosvenor Square. 1937.
Soundly research and rewarding studies. With useful bibliographies.

DYOS, H. J. *Victorian Suburb: A Study of the Growth of Camberwell*. Leicester, 1961.
A pioneer work in the newly-established field of urban studies, based on extensive research into the records of Victorian builders and property developers. The foreword is by Sir John Summerson.

EKWALL, E. *Studies on the Population of Medieval London*. Stockholm, 1956.
Street Names of the City of London. 1954.
The book on the origin and development of the City's street names, by the author of *The Oxford Dictionary of English Place Names*.

ELMES, JAMES. *Metropolitan Improvements; or, London in the 19th Century*. 1827.
Illustrated with engravings based on drawings by Thomas Hosmer Shepherd. In his *Georgian London* Sir John Summerson writes, 'This book is a useful and nearly complete guide to the buildings of George IV's London; for it interprets its title broadly, "improvements" meaning anything from the formation of Regent Street by John Nash to the erection of the School for the Indigent Blind by a Mr Tappen. Behind the book is an apprehension that London, within a matter of fifteen or twenty years, had taken on a new character. And so it had.'

EVANS, GEOFFREY. *Kensington*. 1975.

FITTER, R. S. R. AND LOUSLEY, J. E. *The Natural History of the City*. 1953.

FLETCHER, GEOFFREY. *City Sights*. 1963.
Geoffrey Fletcher, whose drawings appear regularly in the *Daily Telegraph*, has published several collections of his work. These are *Town's Eye View*, *The London Nobody Knows*, *London Overlooked*, *Pearly Kingdom*, and, inevitably, *Dicken's London*. As might be expected from the son of Sir Bannister Fletcher, the architectural details of buildings are a strong feature of his work and repay a careful study.

FRANKLYN, J. *The Cockney: A Survey of London Life and Language*. 1953.

GAUNT, WILLIAM. *Kensington and Chelsea*. 1975.
This is a new and revised omnibus edition of the author's two previous books, *Chelsea* (1954), *Kensington* (1960), with much new material.

GEORGE, M. D. *London Life in the 18th Century*. 1925.
Strong on working class conditions and well-documented. A detailed bibliography.

GIBBS, D. E. W. *Lloyd's of London: A Study of Individualism*. 1957.

GIRAUD, MARK. *Victorian Pubs*. 1975.

GIUSEPPI, J. *The Bank of England*. 1966.
A popular, illustrated history of the 'old lady of Threadneedle Street'.

GODFREY, W. H. *A History of Architecture in and around London*. 1962.
A fine, comprehensive volume devoted to London's architecture with lists of surviving period buildings.

GORDON, W. J. *The Horse World of London*. 1893. Reprinted, 1976.

GOSS, C. W. F. *The London Directories, 1677–1855*. 1932.
A bibliography concerned with their origin and development based on a study of the published directories of the period. Essential reading for anyone trying to trace the history of an old London firm or business.

GREEN, M. AND WHITE, A. J. N. *Guide to London Pubs*. 1968.
Useful for thirsty London pilgrims!

GRIMES, W. F. *The Excavation of Roman and Medieval London*. 1968.
An interim report, as it were, on the excavations which followed the bombing of the City in the Second World War. Deals in great detail with the major investigations like that of Cripplegate Fort, the Temple of Mithras, and some famous old churches like St Bride's off Fleet Street.

GUILDHALL LIBRARY. *London Business House Histories: A Handlist*. 1964.
A classified list of some 8,000 firms' histories, and their original records housed in the Guildhall Library.

The City of London: A Select Booklist. 1972.
Compiled by Donovan Dawe.

HAMILTON, OLIVE AND NIGEL. *Royal Greenwich*. Greenwich, 1969.

HARBEN, H. A. *A Dictionary of London: Being notes Topographical and Historical relating to the Streets and principal Buildings in the City*. 1918.

Still the best historical-topographical dictionary of the City. Fully documented with references to the early forms of the street names. Many maps and plans.

HARPER, CHARLES G. *Queer Things About London: Strange Nooks and Corners of the Greatest City in the World.* 1924.

More Queer Things About London. 1926.

Cycle Rides Round London. 1902.

Like E. Beresford Chancellor, Harper was a prolific *book-maker*, and aside from his *Road* books produced several on London still worth consulting.

HARRIS, CHARLES. *Islington.* 1974.

HARRISON, MICHAEL. *London Beneath the Pavement.* 1971.

A fascinating and quite original exploration of the rivers, sewers, pipes, restaurants, tombs, tunnels, railways and archaeological remains that lie hidden away under our unsuspecting feet.

In the Steps of Sherlock Holmes. Revised edition, Newton Abbot, 1970.

The best book on the London of Sherlock Holmes with copious references to the Conan Doyle stories.

HAYES, JOHN. *Catalogue of the Oil Paintings in the London Museum.* 1970.

A lavishly illustrated and highly-detailed catalogue of the pictures contained, now, in the Museum of London in the City.

HAZLITT, W. C. *The Livery Companies of the City of London: Their Origin, Character, Development, and Social and Political Importance.* 1892.

Still a standard work.

HEAL, SIR AMBROSE. *The London Furniture Makers 1660–1840.* 1953.

An alphabetical list of furniture makers with dates, addresses, and a mass of information gleaned from extensive research.

The London Goldsmiths 1200–1800. Reprinted, Newton Abbot, 1972.

The Signboards of Old London Shops. 1947.

A selection of shop signs mainly from the 17th and 18th centuries.

HERBERT, SIR ALAN P. *The Thames.* 1966.

The name of the author of *The Water Gipsies* should be recommendation enough!

HIBBERT, CHRISTOPHER. *London: The Biography of a City.* 1977.

A beautifully illustrated and elegantly-produced volume. But do not let its glossy coffee-table-look deceive you! Here we have the fruits of a lifetime's research by a professional historian who can also *write*. His book about the Gordon Riots can also be recommended, *King Mob*.

HINDLEY, C. *A History of the Cries of London.* 1884.

Despite many later chatty books on the subject this remains the best researched and the most authoritative.

HOBHOUSE, HERMIONE. *Lost London: A Century of Demolition and Decay.* 1971.

An outspoken and well-documented account with many illustrations of just some of the many London buildings now gone forever.

HOBSON, SIR OSCAR. *How the City Works.* 1966.

An explanation aimed at the average man of how the many financial institutions in the City work. The author takes in clearing banks, merchant banks, insurance companies, Lloyd's, and others.

HOLME, THEA. *The Carlyles at Home.* 1965.

A delightful account, with illustrations by Lynton Lamb, of the home life of Mr and Mrs Thomas Carlyle in Chelsea, when it was merely a small village on the outskirts of London.

HOME, G. C. *Old London Bridge.* 1931.

A history of the bridge up to the time of its demolition in 1832. It includes a chapter on tradesmen's cards by Sir Ambrose Heal, and a list of pictorial records of the old shop-lined bridge. Illustrated.

Medieval London. n.d.

A good work for the general reader, it covers the period AD457–1485. There is a valuable chronology.

JACKSON, A. A. *London's Termini.* Newton Abbot, 1969.

The only satisfactory account of London's main railway termini. Illustrated.

JAMES, E. H. CARKETT. *Her Majesty's Tower of London.* 1953.

A popular history for visitors and others written by the former Resident Governor of the Tower.

JOHNSON, DAVID J. *Southwark and the City.* 1969.

A study in some depth of the City and its relationship with the borough across the Thames.

KELLETT, JOHN R. *The Impact of Railways on Victorian Cities.* 1969.

So much railway literature seems to be aimed at those fascinated by the 'nuts and bolts and huff and puff' of railways, but here is a highly-readable study of the *social* impact of the iron-roads. There is also much useful background material for the lovers of the great Victorian novelists, Dickens, Thackeray, Surtees, and George Eliot.

KENT, WILLIAM. *An Encyclopedia of London.* 1970.

London for Americans. 1950.

London for Everyman. Revised by W. G. Thompson. 1969.

Mine Host London: A Chronicle of Distinguished Visitors. 1948.

Short accounts of famous foreign visitors with selections from their contemporary accounts.

The Lost Treasures of London. 1947.

An illustrated account of the damage caused by the bombing of London between 1939 and 1945.

KNOWLES, DOM DAVID AND GRIMES, W. F. *Charterhouse: The Medieval Foundation in the Light of Recent Discoveries.* 1954.

Largely scaffolded around the story of the exciting post-War archaeological finds on the site of this famous Carthusian monastery. With illustrations and plans.

LIGHT, A. W. *Bunhill Fields.* 2 volumes, Croydon, 1915, 1933.

Brief biographical notes on those buried in this famous cemetery in the City Road opposite John Wesley's Chapel, and described by Robery Southey as 'the Campo Santo of the Noncomformists.'

LILLYWHITE, BRIAN. *London Coffee Houses.* 1963.

A detailed dictionary covering the 17th, 18th and early 19th centuries, with chronological accounts of each and every coffee house. Ideal to have by you when reading Pepys or Evelyn, Boswell or the *Spectator* essays of Addison and Steele.

London Signs: A Reference book of London Signs from the Earliest Times to the Mid-Victorian Era. 1972.

Over 17,000 houses are named, located and dated. Some 19 volumes of additional typescript information have been deposited by the author in the Guildhall Library.

LYSONS, DANIEL. *The Environs of London.* 4 volumes. 1792–7.

Most reference libraries in London have a set of this detailed and well-illustrated work. Invaluable for the London villages that have now been engulfed by the metropolis.

MACKENZIE, GORDON. *Marylebone, Great City North of Oxford Street.* 1972.

Best overall modern history of the area, plenty of good illustrations and a comprehensive bibliography.

MARGETSON, STELLA. *Fifty Years of Victorian London, from the Great Exhibition (1851) to the Queen's Death.* 1969.

MASSINGHAM, H. AND P. *The London Anthology.* 1947.

A pleasant collection of extracts from literary sources covering many aspects of London life, past and present. Some fine contemporary prints are reproduced.

MATTHEWS, W. R. AND ATKINS, WILLIAM (editors). *A History of St Paul's and the Men Associated with it.* 1964.

An impressive symposium covering the Cathedral's history in some depth. Well illustrated.

MAYHEW, HENRY. *London's Underworld.* 1950.

Mayhew's Characters. 1951.

Mayhew's London. n.d.

These three volumes, edited by Peter Quennell, are the best introduction to Mayhew's monumental *London Labour and the London Poor.*

MERRIFIELD, R. *The Roman City of London.* 1965.

Roman London. 1969.

The two works cover the period of the Roman occupation most thoroughly. The later volume is particularly recommended. Both volumes contain many useful bibliographical references.

MITCHELL, R. J. AND LEYS, M. D. R. *A History of London Life.* 1955.

A comprehensive account of London's social life from the earliest days until 1900. Tidily and imaginatively arranged it could be usefully adopted as a text-book for local history studies.

MORLEY, HENRY. *Memoirs of Bartholomew Fair.* 1892.

MORGAN, REVD DEWI. *Phoenix of Fleet Street: 2000 Years of St Bride's.* 1973.

A superbly-produced and illustrated volume on one of the ancient city churches, sadly ruined in the Second World War but now, like a phoenix risen from its own ashes, beautifully restored. The author is the Rector of St Bride's.

NEWTON, DOUGLAS. *Catholic London.* 1950.

A readable survey of London's Catholic associations and history.

NAIRN, IAN. *Nairn's London.* 1966.

Modern Buildings in London. 1964.

The author began writing about architecture in the *Architectural Review* in 1964 and then went on to be *The Observer's* resident watchful eye on new buildings. He has a lively, combative style and really makes one think about architecture. Highly recommended.

OLSEN, DONALD J. *Town Planning in London in the Eighteenth and Nineteenth Centuries.* Yale, 1964.

The most important work on the subject and a model of its kind. Exhaustive notes and references. Illustrated.

PAGE, WALTER. *London: Its Origin and Early Development.* 1929.

Deals with the kingdom and London's place in it until the close of the 12th century. There is some account of the city's growth and much information on the governing families of the period.

PENDRILL, C. *Old Parish Life in London.* 1937.

A detailed account of parish life and administration from the 14th to the 17th century.

PEVSNER, SIR NIKOLAUS. *London: The Cities of London and Westminster.* Revised, 1962.

London: Except the Cities of London and Westminster. Revised, 1962.

These two volumes in the author's superb 'Buildings of England' series cover everything of any architectural interest in the county of London. Indispensable to any serious student of London.

PHILLIPS, HUGH. *The Thames about 1750.* 1951. *Mid-Georgian London.* 1964.
Two beautifully illustrated volumes that are a joy to handle and are as detailed in their coverage as the celebrated *Survey of London.*

PIPER, DAVID. *The Companion Guide to London.* 1964.

PLATTS, BERYL. *A History of Greenwich.* Newton Abbot, 1973.

PRESTIGE, G. L. *St Paul's in its Glory.* 1955.
A domestic account of the Cathedral from 1831 until 1931.

RASMUSSEN, S. E. *London, The Unique City.* 1948.
One of the most exciting books ever written about London, its population, architecture and social life. It is by a Danish architect looking at us with the fresh, objective eyes of a lively, well-informed outsider. It also contains a most useful list of books for further reading.

REDDAWAY, T. F. *The Rebuilding of London after the Great Fire.* 1951.
The best overall account of the rebuilding and the regulations and strictures governing it. Based on original sources and very thorough. Illustrated.

RICHARDSON, A. E. AND GILL, C. L. *London Houses from 1660 to 1820.* n.d.
A useful collection of photographs and plans illustrating the development of London domestic architecture.

RUBINSTEIN, STANLEY. *Historians of London.* 1968.
Not quite the lively and comprehensive volume it should have been.

RUDE, GEORGE. *Hanoverian London 1714–1808.* 1971.
The first of an important new series of period histories of London. Beautifully illustrated and with a detailed bibliography.

SANDS, MOLLIE. *Invitation to Ranelagh 1742–1803.* 1946.
An attractive and scholarly contribution to the study of London's pleasure resorts.

SAUNDERS, HILARY ST GEORGE. *Westminster Hall.* 1951.

SAUNDERS, ANN. *Regent's Park: A Study of the Development of the Area from 1086 to the Present Day,* Newton Abbot, 1969.

SEKON, G. A. *Locomotion in Victorian London.* 1938.

SHEPPARD, F. H. W. *Local Government in St Marylebone 1688–1835: A Study of the Vestry and Turnpike Trust.* 1958.
This rewarding study covers the period during which Marylebone progressed from being a sleepy village on the edge of town to becoming a highly-fashionable residential area, ripe for exploitation in the hands of 19th century developers. A model example of local history.

SHUTE, NERINA. *London Villages.* 1977.

SIMS, J. M. *London and Middlesex Published Records: A Handlist.* 1970.

STAPLETON, A. *London Lanes.* 1930. *London Alleys, Byways and Courts.* 1924.
Two attractive volumes with historical notes and illustrated with pencil drawings by the author.

STENTON, SIR FRANK M. *Norman London.* 1934.
An authoritative study by a fine historian.

STOW, JOHN. *A Survey of London.* 2 volumes, 1971.
This is the best modern edition of the great London classic first published in 1598. Valuable also for the Introduction and notes by C. L. Kingsford.

SUMMERSON, SIR JOHN. *Georgian London.* Revised edition, 1970.
A stimulating and elegantly written work which explains and makes clear how and why London developed in the way that it did between Wren's day and the dawn of the railway age early in the nineteenth century. See also the same author's *John Nash* (1955), *Inigo Jones* (1966), and the earlier *Sir Christopher Wren* (1953).

SURVEY OF LONDON. This magisterial survey of the history of London now runs to about forty volumes.

THOMPSON, F. M. L. *Hampstead: Building a Borough 1650–1964.* 1974.

TIMES, THE. *The History from 1276 to 1956 of the Site in Blackfriars consisting of Printing House Square, &c.* 1956.
This is a handsomely produced volume on the area off Queen Victoria Street surrounding the old offices of *The Times,* earlier the site of a friary of Dominicans (i.e. Black Friars).

TINDALL, GILLIAN. *The Fields Beneath: The History of One London Village.* 1977.
This well-researched study of Kentish Town cannot be praised enough.

WALFORD, EDWARD. *Old and New London: A Narrative of its History, its People, and its Places.* 6 volumes, 1873.
A standard Victorian compilation illustrated with many hundreds of fine illustrations.

WHEATLEY, HENRY B. *London Past and Present.* 3 volumes, 1891.
A monumental work almost beyond criticism, and for the period up until its publication nothing approaches it for scope and sheer information.

WILLIAMS, GUY R. *London in the Country: The Growth of Suburbia.* 1975.

WILLIS, FREDERICK. *A Book of London Yesterdays.* 1960.